SCREENPRINTING
HISTORY AND PROCESS

HOLT, RINEHART AND WINSTON
New York   Chicago   San Francisco   Atlanta   Dallas
Montreal   Toronto   London   Sydney

DONALD SAFF
University of South Florida
DELI SACILOTTO

SCREENPRINTING
HISTORY AND PROCESS

Editor: Rita Gilbert
Picture Editor: Joan Curtis
Developmental Editor: Patricia Gallagher
Project Assistants: Barbara Curialle, Laura Foti
Production Manager: Robert de Villeneuve
Illustrators: Jim Bolles, Abe Markson
Designer: Karen Salsgiver
Associate Designer: Marlene Rothkin Vine
Cover Design: Karen Salsgiver

Chapter 8 revised by Patricia Dreher and Betsy Damos

The authors and publisher give special thanks
to Robert Indiana for the chapter opening images.
They are reprinted from *Numbers*, a book of poetry
by Robert Creeley with plates by Robert Indiana.
Edited by Dr. Dieter Honisch; translated into
German by Klaus Reichert. Publisher: Domberger KG,
Stuttgart/Schmela, Düsseldorf, 1968.

For our parents
Rose and Irving
Alemanna and Olivo

Library of Congress Cataloging in Publication Data

Saff, Donald, 1937–
Screenprinting.

   Bibliography: p. 152
   Includes index.
   1. Screen process printing. I. Sacilotto,
Deli, joint author. II. Title.
TT273.S22   764'.8   78-21877
ISBN 0-03-045491-3

Composition and camera work by York Graphic Services, Inc.,
Pennsylvania. Color separations and printing by Lehigh Press
Lithographers, New Jersey. Printing and binding by Capital
City Press, Vermont.

9 0 1 2 3 138 9 8 7 6 5 4 3 2 1

Preface

Screenprinting is the most accessible and, in some ways, the most contemporary of the four traditional printmaking processes. For this reason, we decided to extract the screenprinting section from our larger book, *Printmaking: History and Process,* and to compile an independent statement about this exciting graphic medium.

Readers familiar with *Printmaking* will find in *Screenprinting* all the information contained in that portion of the larger volume, plus a number of important additions.

The text in *Screenprinting* is written under the assumption that readers have had no previous experience with the medium. Every process stage is illustrated by detailed, step-by-step photographs or drawings in order to clarify the instructions. However, we did not limit ourselves to basic, introductory methods. The book progresses from the simple to the complex, introducing at last the most sophisticated, contemporary techniques.

Screenprinting begins with a brief historical survey, expanded in this volume beyond the treatment in *Printmaking.* Following are chapters devoted to materials and equipment, stencil-making techniques, photographic methods, printing on paper and hard materials, papers for screenprinting, and the curating of prints.

Two completely new chapters have been written for this book. Recognizing the popularity and dynamism of textile screenprinting, we have provided detailed instructions for this medium. Full information is given for adapting the various stencil-making techniques, including photographic methods, to the art fabric. In addition, we have prepared a chapter that lists the chemicals and solvents commonly used in screenprinting, as well as the potential health hazards that may be encountered with these substances.

In assembling the photographic illustrations for *Screenprinting,* we have been especially fortunate. Prominent artists and ateliers across the United States and Canada have made their prints and facilities available to us. Photographs of "works in progress" are just that—important editions actually being printed, rather than demonstration pieces made quickly in the studio for the sake of the book. Some of the most acclaimed artists of the 1970s have generously contributed their advice, details of their methods, and photographs of their work. The finished book contains more than 150 illustrations, 9 of them in full color.

Screenprinting is among the most exciting of the print processes, simply because it lends itself to experimentation with so many types of surfaces—paper, fabric, ceramics, three-dimensional objects of every kind. We have tried to touch upon all of these and, perhaps, smooth the way for artists who will carry the medium into as yet uncharted territory in the years to come.

Acknowledgments

In preparing *Screenprinting: History and Process* we have benefited from the help of a great many people. Our particular thanks go to Norman Lassiter, Ronald J. Lukasiewicz of the University of Georgia, and Denise Mullen of Morris Community College, who read and criticized portions of the material.

We are especially indebted to Patricia Dreher and Betsy Damos, who contributed their expertise to the chapter dealing with printing on textiles. Without their advice, we would not have been able to present such a full statement about the medium.

We are grateful to Sidney Felsen and Stanley Grinstein for giving us access to Gemini G.E.L., and to the Gemini photo archive; to Kathryn Clark and John Clark for providing photographs of the Twinrocker Paper Mill; to Alan Eaker for technical assistance and photographs from Pyramid Arts, Ltd.; to Adolph Rischner and Addie Rischner for permission to photograph works at Styria Studios; to Charles Cardinale of Fine Creations, Inc., for allowing us to photograph work in progress; and to Ian White, Dieter Grund, Charles Fager, and Patrick Lindhardt for technical assistance. We would like to thank Alex Mirzaoff for helping us with the photographic series.

A special note of thanks must go to Robert Rauschenberg and James Rosenquist for allowing us to photograph them at work, as well as for providing the inspiration that made us aim for the highest level of aesthetic excellence.

The staff at Holt, Rinehart and Winston have again been supportive through this new project. Our editor, Rita Gilbert, suggested the solo treatment of screenprinting and encouraged us to expand it beyond its coverage in *Printmaking*. Patricia Gallagher oversaw the production of the book and provided always a charming voice and a sympathetic ear at the other end of the telephone. Picture editor Joan Curtis brought her masterful touch to organizing the illustrations, and Barbara Curialle and Laura Foti kept track of endless production details. We are grateful to Karen Salsgiver for the book's striking, contemporary design and cover, and to Marlene Rothkin Vine for the attractive layout.

Tampa, Florida   Donald Saff
New York   Deli Sacilotto
December 1978

Contents

Process Colors   Four-Color Process Work   **Printing Technique**
Holding the Paper to the Table
Estimating the Amount of Ink Needed   The Flood Stroke
Squeegee Manipulation   Multiple Passes with the Squeegee
Register Guides   Registering on Fully Deckled Paper
Flocked Prints   **Cleaning the Screen**
Removing Direct Emulsion   Removing Presensitized Film
Removing Lacquer Film   Self-Containing Tray
Prints Made with Plastics   Acrylic   *Cutting   Drilling*
Sanding and Polishing   Gluing   Care and Cleaning
Placing Images on Acrylic Sheet   Forming Thermoplastics
Vacuum Forming and Printing   Press Molding
Screenprinting on Ceramics, Metal, or Glass
Printing on Ceramics   Decal Transfer for Ceramics
Printing on Glass   Printing on Metal

The Fabric   The Printing Media   Print Paste Using Pigment
Preparing Pigment Print Paste   Using Pigment Print Pastes   Fixation
Print Paste Using Dye   *Classification of Dyes*
Selecting the Correct Dye   Preparing Dye Print Paste
The Dye Process   *Mixing a Fiber-Reactive Print Paste*
Fixation of Fiber-Reactive Dye
After-Wash of Fabrics Printed with Fiber-Reactive Dye
Screenmaking   Printing Equipment   The Squeegee
The Printing Table   **Preparation for Printing**
Printing the Fabric   Printing with Rail Registration
Printing without Registration Systems   **Safety Precautions**

The Care of Prints   Handling Paper   Trimming Paper
Tearing   Razor Cutting   Matting the Print   Framing the Print

SCREENPRINTING
HISTORY AND PROCESS

Introduction

Since the revitalization of screenprinting by the Pop Art and Op Art movements of the early 1960s, the process has continued to gain in popularity. Bright, sharply defined edges and large-scale photographic imagery are more vividly realized in the screenprinting technique than in the more demanding, more complicated lithographic and intaglio processes. Screenprinting also is easy to learn and simple to do. Colors and screens can be changed readily, and the printing itself is fast and relatively effortless. One of the most versatile of printmaking techniques, screenprinting is suitable for both sharp, crisp images and fluid, painterly effects (Fig. 1; Pl. 1, p. 15). Because almost every technique used in screenprinting reproduces the image in positive form (as opposed to a reversed or negative image), the method offers great advantages in allowing the artist to assess the work accurately in various stages during the printing process.

There is a considerable difference between the beginner and the professional screenprinter, but the image-making and printing procedures remain simple. The necessary materials are inexpensive. No heavy machinery is needed. Much can be done with just a sturdy table, a few screens, a squeegee, inks, and a simple drying arrangement for the prints. If the image-making procedures become more exacting and involved, however, more sophisticated equipment (such as a vacuum table) is needed.

1. **James Rosenquist.** *Miles.* 1975.
Screenprint with airbrushed rainbow,
30 × 22″ (75 × 55 cm).
Courtesy Graphicstudio,
University of South Florida, Tampa.

Screenprinting is a variation of the stencil process. In stenciling, a shape cut from a piece of dense paper is recreated on another surface by dabbing ink or paint through the cut-out. In screenprinting, fabric stretched tightly on a rigid frame becomes the screen, or support, for the stencil. A stencil is made either by painting a substance (such as glue) onto the fabric, or by adhering a special film to the screen that prevents ink from passing through. One controls the areas that print by controlling the parts of the screen that remain open to the free passage of ink.

Screen ink is highly viscous and will not flow through the screen by itself. The rubber or plastic blade of a squeegee must be pulled across the fabric to force the ink through the open areas.

The term *silkscreening* is sometimes used because silk is the traditional support fabric, although other materials such as nylon and polyester are now more common. Another term for the process, *serigraphy,* is derived from the Latin word *seri,* silk, and the Greek *graphos,* to write.

ONE

A Brief History of Screenprinting

Screenprinting is among the newest of the graphic arts, with a relatively short history as a fine-art medium. Nevertheless, the origin of the technique itself is still quite obscure. There is little doubt that the process owes much to the ancient and simple stencil methods practiced throughout many parts of the world (Fig. 2). Early stencils and pigments were made from organic materials and so have not survived to the present.

More precisely documented are the applications of stenciling developed in China and Japan between A.D. 500 and 1000. The Chinese and Japanese found the process well suited for transferring images to fabric (Fig. 3), as a means of decoration as well as for making embroidery patterns. The cutout stencil allowed the heavy deposition of dye and pigments so necessary for textile printing. In addition to satisfying these practical needs, stenciling also was considered an art form in itself in the East.

The technique probably reached the West through the journeys of Marco Polo in the late 13th and early 14th centuries, when so many new ideas and materials were flooding Europe. It was still a relatively crude method at best, suitable only for bold shapes and patterns. One of the main drawbacks was that images could be produced if the cut shapes remained attached to and were supported by the stencil matrix itself. The difficulty of introducing floating shapes was apparent—a separate piece could not be used without changing its position or lifting off the surface. With the opening of

2. Prehistoric negative handprints.
Pech-Merle, c. 15,000–10,000 B.C.
Lot, France.

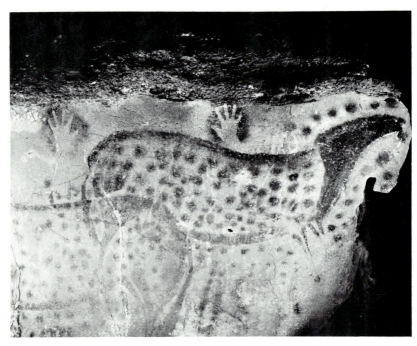

3. Japanese stencil used to decorate silk.
c. 1680–1750, Tokugawa period.
Slater Memorial Museum,
Norwich Free Academy, Norwich, Conn.
(Vanderpoel Collection).

Japan to Westerners by the journeys of Commodore Matthew Perry
in the mid-1850s, it was discovered that the Japanese had solved this
problem long since.

The Japanese had perfected a method of using fine silk threads
and strands of human hair to hold the floating shapes in place,
allowing intricate patterns of almost unlimited complexity to be
made. The strands of hair or silk were attached to the surface of the
stencil matrix at intervals of about $\frac{1}{4}$ inch. They extended in many
directions and served to support the delicate, floating shapes. An
identical stencil was placed on top, sealing the fibers firmly in

position. The entire stencil was then varnished and flattened, forming the first direct precursor of the modern screen. Color was dabbed through the open areas with a stiff brush, yielding continuous patterns unimpeded by the thin threads and reproducing only the basic shapes.

Screenprinting on Fabric

Silk as a stencil carrier probably was used in France about 1870 for the printing of textiles. The first *imprimés à la Lyonnaise* were produced on silk at Lyons. These were very costly, and their market, consequently, was small and exclusive. The process later spread to Switzerland and Germany but on a limited basis.

England, which had very stringent and well-documented patent laws, recorded the use of a silk stencil in a patent awarded to Samuel Simson of Manchester in 1907. Printing through the stenciled silk was done with a stiff bristle brush. The introduction of the squeegee later speeded up the process and also produced a more even layer of ink. Paul Pilsworth used Simson's method in 1915 to produce banners for the United States Army. However, it was not until experiments in the United States in the early 1900s suggested the economic possibilities for screenprinting that the method became generally accepted. Each succeeding patent improved the quality of the technique: photographic screens (1915 and 1921), carbon tissue stencil screens (1920), a screenprinting press (1921), a screen stenciling press for textiles (1925), and the stencil film process (1930). France is credited with having established the first commercial screenprinting on bulk fabric in 1926. During the next decade in many parts of Europe and the United States screenprinting on bulk fabric became popular in the furniture textile trade. As screens and dyes improved, the process was used for the dress fabric market as well.

Before screenprinting, most fabric was printed using engraved rollers or hand blocks—a difficult and costly process. Rollers and blocks are expensive, while screens are relatively easy and cheap to produce. This economy of production encouraged experimentation and increased the freedom of the designer. Any type of design could be reproduced exactly to the smallest detail.

The Great Depression of the 1930s brought about higher costs for fabric and lower demand for designer fabric, so it became apparent that a cheaper method for printing fabrics must be developed. Screenprinting provided the technique. Even when the economy improved, the screen process remained in favor, because it successfully met the needs of changing fashions.

Among the well-known artists designing for the first manufacturers to use screenprinting on a large basis were Duncan Grant, Vanessa Bell, Paul Nash, Hans Lisdale, Marion Dorn, Michael O'Connell, and Ben Nicholson. The fabric design of Henry Moore

4. Henry Moore.
Two Standing Figures. 1949.
Screenprint on linen,
9′4″ × 6′ (2.85 × 1.83 m).
Courtesy Marlborough Fine Art Ltd., London.

5. Maija Isola. *Silkkikuikka.*
Screenprint on cotton.
© Marimekko Oy 1961.

(Fig. 4) was shown at an exhibition arranged by the Cotton Board in England. Other exhibitions by other well-known artists followed, and in 1953 the *Ambassador* magazine held an exhibition called "Paintings into Textures" at the Institute of Contemporary Arts in England, in which Henry Moore and William Gear showed screenprinted fabrics.

The nature of screenprinting encouraged designers to work without restrictions, since any design could be reproduced exactly. The process also lent itself to translations from other printing methods. A photographically prepared screen could easily reproduce designs made from batik, tie-dye, block and roller prints, and any graphic work.

In the 1950s and 1960s fabric came to be treated as a canvas, and design indistinguishable from contemporary art was applied to it. A fashion developed early in the 1960s for large floral designs, because screens could carry much larger designs (or *repeats*) than rollers. There were also abstract paintings on cloth in 5- or 6-foot repeats (Fig. 5).

Screenprinting mechanization has moved so fast, that often companies do not have the finances to reequip their shops as often as they would like. Firms in Germany and Switzerland, however, have made great advances in automatic screenprinting. The two major categories of equipment are the flatbed and the rotary printer. In the former, screens follow one another down long tables of 40 or more yards (Fig. 6). These tables proved more economical for short runs than the older machines, which had used wooden rollers with the design raised in felt and outlined in copper. In a development of this method, the screens stayed still and the fabric moved beneath them. This method allowed for production of 160 yards of cloth in 10 colors per hour, and the table could be shortened to 4 or 5 yards.

In about 1964 one of Europe's biggest textile machinery manufacturers, the Stork Company of Holland, developed a new form of rotary screen printer. This machine prints color through a constantly rotating cylindrical screen. A cylindrical screen, in contrast to a flat screen, can maintain a steady motion, rather than an intermittent one, and can print at speeds up to 2400 yards per hour. The rotating screenprinter also can print up to 24 colors. Cylindrical metal screens are mounted horizontally along the machine and revolve in contact with an endless belt, which carries the cloth into a large dryer (Fig. 7). An automatic level controls the rate at which the colors are poured into each screen, and this rate is determined by the requirements of the design.

above: 6.
Flatbed screenprinting operation.
Courtesy Fibers Division,
Allied Chemical Corp.

left: 7.
Rotary screenprinting operation.
Courtesy Fibers Division,
Allied Chemical Corp.

One effect of the collaboration between artist and industrialist is the integration of design, fabric, and sophisticated technology. This cooperation has fostered a number of screenprinting developments. In automatic screenprinting systems it is now possible to use just a few screens to produce a wide variety from limited themes. Spraying techniques—which can be as simple as directing a spray gun through a stencil onto the fabric—permit shaded areas. By using stencil screens with mechanized controls or electronically controlled spray lines, this technique could be further enhanced. Color change and shading could also be automatically controlled. These along with other innovations make the variety of textile designs infinite.

Screenprinting as a Graphic Medium

The applications of the screenprinting technique in the early 20th century were largely commercial. Screenprinting proved to be a perfect medium for the bold designs and colors that appealed to a burgeoning advertising industry. In particular, a new phenomenon—the billboard—owed its proliferation to silkscreen techniques. Cylindrical bottles, cans, and other oddly shaped items could be screenprinted as well, and as time went on, new developments in electronics showed that screen methods could be employed for printed circuitry of all kinds.

During the height of the Depression, a Works Progress Administration (WPA) screenprinting project was begun under the direction of the artist and printmaker Anthony Velonis (Fig. 8). By 1935 Velonis and his group were able for the first time to bring the screen process to the attention of serious artists. Many rejected the creative possibilities of screenprinting, largely because of the heavily commercial character it bore at that time. In order to differentiate creative screen work from the more mundane purposes the process served, Carl Zigrosser, then curator of the Philadelphia Museum of Fine Arts, coined the term *serigraph*.

In the late 1920s, Louis D'Autremont in Dayton, Ohio, developed a knife-cut shellac stencil material called Profilm. The ease with which sharp-edge stencils could now be adhered to the screen changed the medium. Later, after Joseph Ulano improved the film and introduced both a lacquer stencil material and a gelatin photosensitive material, screenprinting was able to keep pace with other graphic processes.

The National Serigraph Society was formed in 1940. This group exhibited screenprints throughout the world, emphasizing the creative aspects of the technique. Serigraphy soon became part of the vocabulary of graphic art, as museums added prints to their collections and in turn promoted the artistic legitimacy of the process. Initially, many of the WPA Art Project-sponsored prints imitated crayon drawings, watercolors, and oil paintings. During the period from 1935 to 1950, however, a considerable number of artists accepted the process for their own work and began to explore its particular characteristics. Harry Sternberg, Guy Maccoy, Hyman

9. Harry Sternberg.
Robert Gwathmey. 1944.
Screenprint, $18\frac{3}{8} \times 12\frac{5}{8}''$ (47 × 32 cm).
New York Public Library,
Prints Division
(Astor, Lenox, and Tilden Foundations).

10. Elizabeth Olds.
Tourists. 1933–39.
Screenprint, $9\frac{1}{2} \times 15''$ (24 × 38 cm).
New York Public Library,
Prints Division
(Astor, Lenox, and Tilden
Foundations).

11. Ben Shahn.
Where There is a Book
There is No Sword. 1950.
Screenprint printed in black,
$13\frac{7}{8} \times 11\frac{5}{8}''$ (35 × 29 cm).
Museum of Modern Art, New York.

Worsager, Elizabeth Olds, Loris Bunce, Mervin Jules, Edward London, Ruth Gikow, Ben Shahn, and Velonis himself led the way (Figs. 9–11). In the 1950s the technique was further explored and adapted to more personal kinds of imagery, including that of the artist Marcel Duchamp (Fig. 12).

By the 1960s screenprinting had been adopted wholesale in the commercial printing industry (Fig. 13). Its use for art prints was fostered by such influential figures as the English printer Christo-

12. Marcel Duchamp. *Self-Portrait.* 1959.
Screenprint printed in blue,
7⅞″ (20 cm) square.
Museum of Modern Art, New York
(gift of Lang Charities, Inc.).

13. Automated screenprinting press.
Courtesy Lehigh Press.

14. R. B. Kitaj.
The Romance of the Civil Service
(Charge Sheet). 1967. Screenprint,
$40\frac{1}{4} \times 26\frac{7}{8}''$ (102 × 68 cm).
Courtesy Marlborough Gallery, Inc., New York.

15. Eduardo Paolozzi.
*A Formula That Can Shatter
into a Million Glass Bullets.*
1967. Screenprint.
Courtesy Pace Editions, Inc., New York.

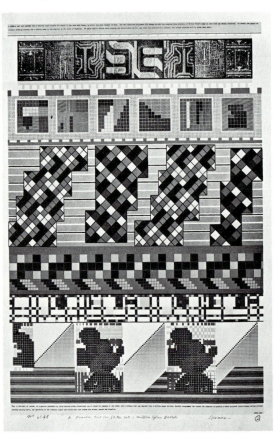

pher Prater. Prater began his career as a commercial printer, but he later produced works for such artists as R. B. Kitaj and Eduardo Paolozzi (Figs. 14, 15).

Screenprinting proved ideal for the aesthetic movements of the 1960s. Possibly because of the close relationship to commercial printing methods, the medium lent itself naturally to the popular or "Pop" art imagery of such artists as Andy Warhol, Jasper Johns, and Roy Lichtenstein (Figs. 16–18), who transformed recognizable symbols of American culture into new artistic statements.

16. Andy Warhol. *Campbell's.* 1964.
Screenprint on wood,
$10 \times 19 \times 9\frac{1}{2}''$ (25 × 47 × 24 cm).
Courtesy Leo Castelli, Inc.,
New York.

Plate 1. Michael Heizer. *Untitled*, from *Lashonda* series. 1975. Painting through screen over a black silkscreened element, 42″ (105 cm) square. Courtesy Gemini G.E.L., Los Angeles.

Plate 3. Roy Lichtenstein.
Moonscape, from *11 Pop Artists*, Volume I. 1967.
Screenprint, 12 × 18¹/₁₆″ (30 × 45 cm).
Museum of Modern Art, New York
(gift of Original Editions).

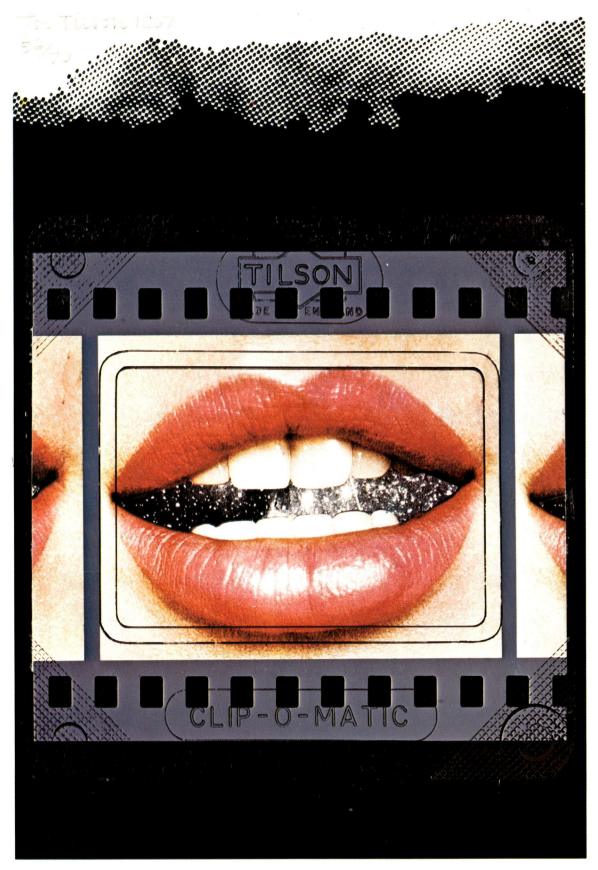

Plate 4. Joe Tilson. *Transparency, Clip-O-Matic Lips 2.* 1967–68.
Screenprint on acetate film with metalized acetate film, 34¾ × 25⅞″ (87 × 65 cm). Tate Gallery, London.

17. Jasper Johns.
Flags I. 1973.
31-color screenprint,
$27\frac{3}{8} \times 35\frac{3}{8}''$ (68 × 88 cm).
Courtesy Leo Castelli, Inc., New York.

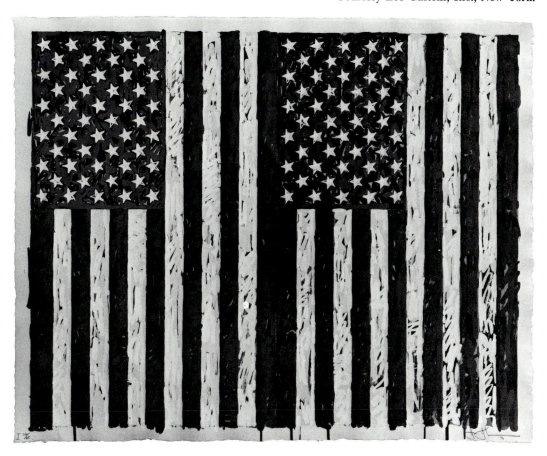

18. Roy Lichtenstein.
Untitled, from *Six Still Lifes.*
1974. Screenprint and lithograph,
$35\frac{7}{8} \times 44\frac{3}{4}''$ (90 × 112 cm).
Courtesy Multiples, Inc., New York.

Screenprinting as a Graphic Medium   **19**

One of the greatest advantages of the screen technique is the relative ease of multiple-color printing. A screenprinting workshop is not expensive to set up and requires fewer skills on the part of the printer than other methods. Virtually any paper can be used for printing, making this method more accessible than any other print medium. In addition, the colors are more predictable than in other types of printmaking, since the inks tend to be opaque and ride on the surface of the paper. Thus, when artists of the mid-20th century

19. Ellsworth Kelly.
Black and Red. 1970.
Screenprint, $24\frac{7}{8} \times 30''$ (62×75 cm).
Courtesy Leo Castelli, Inc.,
New York.

20. Victor Vasarely.
Untitled, from the portfolio
CTA 102. 1966.
Color screenprint,
$27\frac{3}{4}''$ (69 cm) square.
Museum of Modern Art, New York
(John S. Newberry Fund).

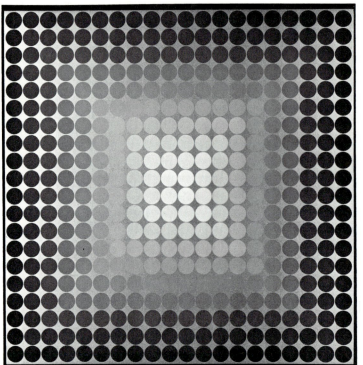

began to concentrate on color as the actual subject of their works—in the broad areas of Color Field painting or the vibrating harmonies of optical art—screenprinting again served as a natural medium for adaptation to prints (Figs. 19, 20). The flat colors and precise, ruler-sharp edges of "hard-edge" painting and Minimal Art also translated readily and easily into screenprinting, since they are characteristics integral to the stencil process (Figs. 21, 22; Pl. 2, p. 16; Pl. 7, p. 93).

left: 21. Ernest Trova.
Print #4, from Series Seventy-Five.
1975. Screenprint,
42 × 35″ (105 × 87 cm).
Courtesy Pace Editions, Inc., New York.

below: 22. Will Barnet.
Aurora. 1977.
Screenprint, 17½ × 40″
(44 × 102 cm).
Courtesy the artist.

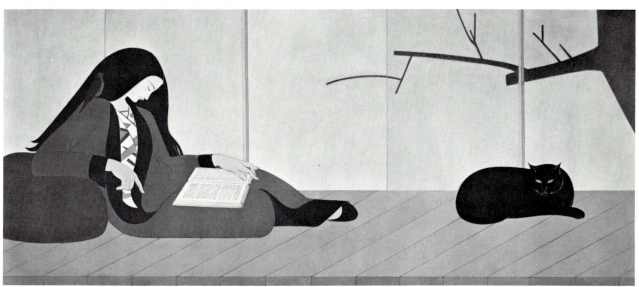

Indicative of the combined and expanded methods that many artists have investigated are Robert Rauschenberg's *Star Quarters* (Pl. 9, p. 94); James Rosenquist's *Earth and Moon* (Fig. 115); Roy Lichtenstein's *Moonscape,* printed on metallic plastic (Pl. 3, p. 17); Brice Marden's *Painting Study II,* printed with heated encaustics (Fig. 23); Joe Tilson's *Transparency, Clip-O-Matic Lips 2,* on acetate film with metalized acetate film (Pl. 4, p. 18); and Anuszkiewicz' mammoth screenprint on masonite, *Blue to Red Portal* (Pl. 5, p. 59). Screenprinting lends itself especially well to combination with other media, including painting, collage, and sculpture (Fig. 26).

Recent Fine Arts Applications

Screenprinting has witnessed an astonishing variety of applications in conjunction with innovative use of papers, plastics, photographs, and fabrics. The technique of screenprinting on large canvas works has been used by Robert Rauschenberg and Andy Warhol since the 1950s (Fig. 24). On a smaller scale, Lucas Samaras has mixed a variety of media—offset lithography, silkscreen, thermography, embossing, and diecutting—to create his 98-color, ten-page *Book* (Fig. 25). In Claes Oldenburg's *Soft Drum Set* (Fig. 26) screenprint

23. Brice Marden.
Painting Study II. 1974.
Screenprint with wax
and graphite applications.
Courtesy Multiples, Inc., New York.

24. Andy Warhol.
American Indian Series. 1976.
Screenprint on canvas,
3′6″ × 4′2″ (1.05 × 1.25 m).
Tehran Museum of Contemporary Art.

below: **25.**
Lucas Samaras. *Book.* 1968.
98-color multimedia work,
10 × 10 × 2″ (25 × 25 × 5 cm).
Courtesy Pace Editions, Inc.,
New York.

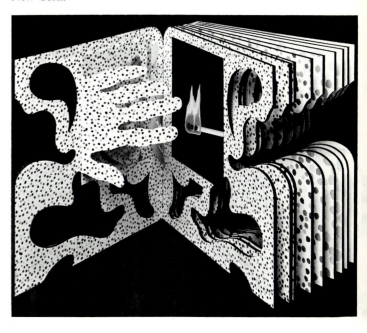

26. Claes Oldenburg.
Soft Drum Set. 1969. Soft sculpture
with screenprinted canvas and wood,
10 × 19 × 14″ (25 × 47 × 35 cm).
Courtesy Multiples, Inc., New York.

27. James Rosenquist.
Coins in Space for Daniel Ellsberg. 1972.
Screenprint on fabric and vinyl,
8′2″ × 5′5″ (2.45 × 1.63 m).
Courtesy Multiples, Inc., New York.

below: 28. Ed Ruscha.
Fruit-Metrecal Hollywood. 1971.
Screenprint, 10 × 37½″ (25 × 94 cm).
Courtesy Cirrus Editions, Ltd., Los Angeles.

techniques were applied to fabrics, which were in turn sewn onto a three-dimensional object.

James Rosenquist's *Coins in Space for Daniel Ellsberg* (Fig. 27), produced on fabric at Styria Studios, employed a large-scale gradated or rainbow roll, a technique usually associated with smaller-scale works on paper. The large squeegee was fitted with a partitioned ink reservoir that maintained the proximity and integrity of the colors. Ed Ruscha dispensed with commercially prepared ink and used Metrecal with grape and apricot jam to print his silkscreened *Fruit-Metrecal Hollywood* (Fig. 28), physically uniting content and material. The prints, surprisingly, have remained colorfast with the message intact.

The reappearance of the figure in 20th-century art coincided in time with the trend toward increasing numbers of colors in screen work, and these two elements complement each other (Fig. 29). With the advent of Photorealism, works in ten, twenty, or more colors can reproduce with photographic accuracy the figurative imagery of this style (Fig. 30). It should be clear that this medium has become an indispensable part of the artistic vocabulary of the times, and a valuable form of expression.

above: **29. Alex Katz.** *Good Morning.* 1975.
9-color screenprint, $37\frac{1}{2} \times 28\frac{1}{2}''$ (94 × 71 cm).
Courtesy Brooke Alexander, Inc., New York.

below: **30. Audrey Flack.** *Royal Flush.* 1977.
Screenprint, $4' \times 5'6''$ (1.22 × 1.68 m).
Courtesy Louis K. Meisel Gallery, New York.

TWO

Materials
and Equipment

The Basic Frame

The following materials are needed for constructing and preparing the frame and the screen:

o wood or aluminum frame, handmade or readymade
o screen fabric (silk, nylon, or polyester)
o nylon or polyester tape
o staple gun
o stretching pliers (optional)
o powdered cleanser, powdered pumice, or No. 400 carborundum
o nylon scrub brush
o Screen Prep or Mesh Prep (optional)
o gummed brown paper tape, $2\frac{1}{2}$ to 3 inches wide
o epoxy resin (optional)
o drop stick or other lifting device
o baseboard of plywood, Novaply, or Formica

Joining the Frame

The first step in preparing to make a screenprint is to obtain the frame that holds the screen. Although inexpensive readymade frames can be purchased, it is a simple job to make your own. The most common material for the frame is wood, usually pine or

31. Before constructing the frame,
determine the size of the image
and leave room for the squeegee and the ink.

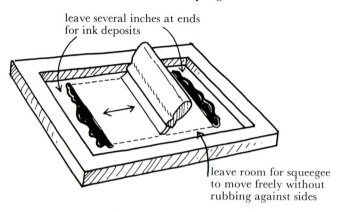

leave several inches at ends
for ink deposits

leave room for squeegee
to move freely without
rubbing against sides

32. The butt joint for attaching
the sides of the frame.

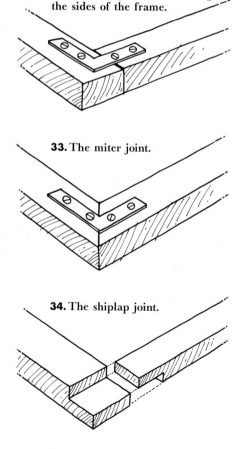

33. The miter joint.

34. The shiplap joint.

35. The tongue-and-groove joint.

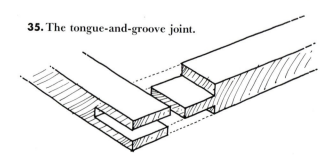

spruce. (Aluminum frames, considerably more expensive than their wooden counterparts, are available commercially. Although some have built-in devices for stretching the fabric, they offer few advantages in either weight or performance, except that they can be immersed in special cleaning tanks unsuitable for wooden frames.)

The wood used for the frame must be straight, smooth, and free of knots, and thoroughly dry. The thickness of the wood will depend on the size of the screen. For example, a small frame measuring 12 by 16 inches could be made from 1-by-2-inch stock. A larger, 36-by-48-inch frame requires wood at least $1\frac{1}{2}$ inches square or even larger. For bigger frames, 2-by-2-inch lumber is usually adequate.

Before you actually construct the frame, consider the size of the printing area. The frame should be at least $1\frac{1}{2}$ inches larger on the sides than the printing area, and at least 3 inches larger at either end. This allows room for the squeegee to travel and permits printing ink to be deposited at either end of the screen (Fig. 31). It is sometimes a good idea to leave margins of 3 to $3\frac{1}{2}$ inches between the inside of the frame and the beginning of the image on all four sides, particularly on screens larger than 24 by 30 inches. This will allow the image to be printed either horizontally or vertically, and the squeegee to be drawn in either direction.

Any one of several types of joints can be used for securing the corners of the frame, such as the *butt joint, miter joint, shiplap joint,* and *tongue-and-groove joint* (Figs. 32–35). Whichever joint is used, it is most important that the pieces of wood meet *exactly*. There must be no twisting and no uneven surfaces. The entire frame—especially the side on which the fabric is to be stretched—should be smooth and should lie perfectly flat. Bumps in the wood, jagged edges, and rough surfaces should be sanded down before the fabric is stretched, to prevent tearing it. The frame should also be rigid enough to withstand the tension of a tightly stretched screen without warping or bending.

Screen Fabrics and Their Characteristics

The traditional screen fabric, silk, has been used much less in the last decade than formerly. This is due in part to the tremendous improvement in the quality of synthetic fabrics. Nylon and polyester fabrics are ideal for use with direct photo emulsions, which are now more frequently employed in screenprinting than ever before. For direct tusche or litho crayon techniques, silk is preferred.

Silk   Silk for screenprinting is a *multifilament* fabric; that is, each strand is composed of innumerable, finer strands (Fig. 36). This allows great adhesion of all kinds of stencils to the screen, including photographic film and handcut film. Silk has excellent dimensional stability and good wearing qualities, and is available in a variety of types. The finest grade is Swiss-made, although domestic and Japanese silk are adequate for most of the techniques in which silk is preferred. Silk is unaffected by solvents such as lacquer thinner, alcohol, benzine, mineral spirits, and turpentine. Once stretched, it will remain tight on the frame, being only slightly affected by humidity. (It loosens slightly when wet, but tightens when dry.)
    Silk is excellent for drawings made directly on the screen and for indirect photo emulsions (such as Ulano Hi-Fi Green or Blue). The

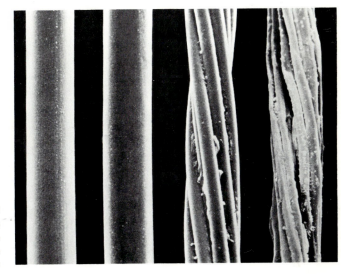

36. Left to right: monofilament nylon, monofilament polyester, multifilament polyester, and multifilament silk.

latter can be removed easily from the silk by spraying with hot water, and/or by soaking in an enzyme cleaner. Since silk is an organic material, it can be destroyed by strong acids and alkalies. For this reason, it is unsuitable for repeated use with direct photo emulsions, which are removed with bleach.

Nylon   Nylon is a most durable material, capable of withstanding great punishment and extremely hard use. The nylon used in screenprinting is a *monofilament* fabric, whose horizontal and vertical threads are made of a single strand of nylon (Fig. 36). The greatest drawback of nylon is its elasticity. It stretches considerably when wet, and tightens again as it dries. It is even affected by humid weather. This tendency must be taken into consideration whenever close color registration is needed, especially on large screens where even the slightest misalignment becomes apparent.

Nylon fabric can be used safely with most solvents, such as lacquer thinner, benzine, mineral spirits, alcohol, and turpentine, but not with strong acids.

Polyester   Polyester fabrics are among the newest and most versatile of the synthetics. They are available in both multifilament and monofilament form and are excellent for all techniques. Polyesters have excellent dimensional stability and high tensile strength, allowing them to be stretched tightly even on very large screens and to be used in situations that require critical registration. Polyester is much less easily affected by humidity than either silk or nylon and combines some of the best features of both. It is impervious to strong alkalies and acids and can be used safely with lacquer thinner, alcohol, benzine, mineral spirits, and turpentine. Like silk, multifilament polyester is ideal for hand-drawn images.

Classification of Screen Fabrics

The weight and fineness of silk and multifilament polyester are expressed in terms of a number followed by an X, XX, or XXX. A single X indicates standard weight. The weight most often used for screenprinting is XX, or double extra weight. An XXX size indicates that there is an extra strand in both the lengthwise threads (the *warp*) and the crosswise threads (the *woof*), giving added strength and wearing ability.

Mesh sizes range from 6XX to 25XX, and the higher the number, the finer the mesh. An 8XX fabric has 86 strands of fabric per inch; a 20XX fabric, 175 threads per inch. The average mesh size for most work is about 12XX to 14XX. For textile printing, however, the fabric most often used has a rating of about 8XX or 10XX. These screens have a great percentage of open area in the fabric and allow the passage of the heavy layer of ink necessary for textile printing.

Comparison of Mesh Sizes

Natural Silk

number	mesh count per inch	mesh opening in inches
6XX	74	.0096
8XX	86	.0076
10XX	105	.0063
12XX	124	.0047
14XX	139	.0039
16XX	157	.0035
18XX	171	.0032
25XX	195	.0025

Multifilament Polyester

number	mesh count per inch	mesh opening in inches	open area %	fabric thickness in inches
6XX	74	.0092	44	.0061
8XX	86	.0071	36	.0059
10XX	110	.0051	30	.0051
12XX	125	.0045	27	.0047
14XX	137	.0042	26	.0047
16XX	158	.0035	27	.0039
20XX	175	.0033	36	.0035
25XX	196	.0028	31	.0033

Monofilament Nylon

mesh count per inch	mesh opening in inches	open area %	fabric thickness in inches
74	.0077	34	.0106
86	.0076	44	.0072
109	.0055	37	.0071
124	.0050	42	.0055
140	.0044	38	.0049
160	.0035	32	.0052
180	.0032	31	.0042
200	.0030	36	.0033
235	.0024	31	.0033
260	.0021	31	.0030
285	.0021	31	.0030
306	.0018	29	.0027
330	.0017	34	.0024
355	.0016	33	.0024
380	.0014	30	.0023
420	.0010	18	.0026
457	.0010	21	.0023

Monofilament Polyester

mesh count per inch	mesh opening in inches	open area %	fabric thickness in inches
54	.0124	44	.0118
64	.0106	42	.0094
74	.0087	42	.0094
86	.0075	46	.0073
110	.0059	43	.0057
125	.0051	42	.0049
140	.0047	42	.0045
160	.0038	35	.0047
180	.0035	38	.0039
200	.0028	29	.0045
235	.0024	31	.0039
260	.0022	31	.0030
285	.0020	32	.0029
306	.0017	27	.0029
335	.0016	25	.0022
350	.0012	19	.0029
380	.0013	24	.0026
420	.0010	18	.0026

The percentage of open area is, in effect, an efficiency rating for the fabric. The greater the open area, the greater the ink flow through the fabric. When a very fine mesh is employed that also has a comparatively high percentage of open area, the diameter of each strand of fabric is necessarily finer. This is important in halftone printing, in which maximum detail and a minimum of interference from the screen fabric are required. See the table above.

Screen fabrics are sold by the yard in bolts ranging from 40 inches to over 6 feet in width. When calculating the amount of fabric to buy, allow for 2 to 3 extra inches beyond the dimensions of the frame.

Stretching the Fabric

One of the most important factors in good printing is the tightness of the fabric on the frame. Any slack will cause blurred images and make close registration impossible. The larger the screen, the more important it is to have a taut fabric, since any degree of slack becomes magnified over a greater distance as the squeegee exerts a pulling force during printing. In multicolor printing requiring several different screens, it is important to have the tensions of all the screens as close to one another as possible.

Moisture affects all screen fabrics even after the fabric has been stretched, making the screen slightly tighter on dry days and looser on humid days. As a result, if the fabric is wet before being stretched, a tighter screen will result thereby minimizing this effect.

The groove-and-cord method of stretching the fabric on the screen is used on many commercially made frames. The frame has a groove all around the bottom, over which the fabric is placed. The grooves must be smoothed with sandpaper to avoid catching the fabric. A cord pushed into the groove holds the fabric firmly in place. The fabric can be tightened by forcing the cord farther into the groove. To change the fabric, simply remove the cord.

One of the finest methods for stretching the fabric involves the M & M Fabric Stretcher, with a series of pneumatically operated stretching units. In this technique, utilized by many professional printers for fine detail and process printing, the fabric is stretched over the frame simultaneously from all sides by the stretcher. The tension is equalized all around, and the degree of tension is monitored by a dialed pressure gauge. This allows for the maximum tension for a given type of fabric and also ensures an identical degree of tension on two or more screens, aiding registration. After the fabric has been stretched, it is adhered to the frame with epoxy. The tension is maintained until the epoxy has hardened. This method of stretching has proven ideal for situations in which consistency and close tolerances are demanded, particularly when used with polyester screens.

All the stretching can be done by hand. On very large screens, however, stretching pliers will help give the necessary tension to the fabric if your grip is weak.

Because of its unique characteristics, nylon is best stretched in stages. It should be wet with water and stretched until taut. The process should be repeated several times until a maximum point of tension has been reached. Polyester needs to be stretched only once. Silk should be scrubbed with detergent and water, then rinsed well.

37. Staple the first side
of the fabric to the bottom
of the frame.

This removes the sizing and results in a tighter screen. New wooden frames should be weighted to prevent warping as they dry.

Stapling the Fabric to the Frame

If you are stretching your fabric by hand, cut the fabric, if possible, so that it is at least 2 inches larger than the outside dimensions of the frame. Lay it over the frame, making sure that the threads run parallel to the sides of the frame. Next, staple the edge of the fabric to the bottom of the frame, pulling it evenly in the direction of the stapling (Fig. 37).

A special strong fabric tape made of polyester or nylon is available for use with this method. The tape is placed over the fabric so that both it and the fabric are stapled simultaneously. When the fabric is to be removed from the frame, the tape is stripped from the edge, pulling all the staples with it.

Staple at an angle rather than parallel to the frame; this prevents tearing of the fabric when the tension is increased. When the first side has been completed, pull the fabric to the opposite side, and put three or four staples about an inch or so apart in the center of the frame (Fig. 38). Next, staple the other two sides at the center, being careful to pull the fabric tightly and evenly all around. Pull and staple each side in rotation, working from the center, and placing a few staples at a time until all sides have been completed (Fig. 39). A space of about ¾ inch should be left between the staples the first time around the frame. Further tightening can be done by pulling the fabric and stapling between the staples already on the

38. Place a few staples in the center of the opposite side.

39. After tacking down the centers
of the other two sides, staple all the way around.
Extra staples can be added to tighten the fabric.

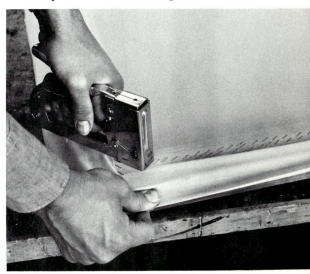

40. Press the gummed tape firmly over the staples so that it extends about ¾ inch onto the screen.

41. Turn the frame over and tape the inside, covering both wood and fabric.

frame. Finally, hammer the staples into the frame so that they are flush with the surface.

Cleaning the Stretched Fabric

After it has been stretched, the fabric should be given a "tooth," so that all types of stencils will adhere to the smooth strands of fabric. There are a few ways of doing this. Special preparations for nylon are available, such as Screen Prep or Mesh Prep, which are scrubbed onto the surface with water. Another method that also can be used for monofilament and multifilament polyester fabrics is to scrub both sides of the fabric with powdered cleanser, powdered pumice, or No. 400 carborundum and a little detergent, using water and a nylon brush. The fabric should always be rinsed thoroughly with clean water afterwards, particularly if it is multifilament polyester. This removes all traces of powder or detergent from the strands. It is a good idea to prepare the screen in this way the first two or three times the screen is used to ensure that the fabric will hold the stencil.

Taping the Screen

Once you have stretched and cleaned the fabric, the next step is to tape the edges of the screen. This prevents ink from seeping through the ends of the fabric and getting on the margins of the print. It also eliminates the problem of ink being pushed in between the frame and the end of the fabric, only to appear during the printing of another color. Taping also facilitates the process of cleaning up once the printing has been completed.

The most convenient tape is ordinary gummed, brown paper tape, between $2\frac{1}{2}$ and 3 inches wide. Cut four strips of tape, equal in length to the four sides of the frame. Moisten the gummed side with water, and apply the tape to the underside of the frame, so that it covers the tacks or staples and extends $\frac{3}{4}$ inch or so onto the screen. Press the moistened tape down firmly (Fig. 40). Cut four more strips, then turn the frame over and adhere these to the inside of the frame, so that the tape covers both the fabric and the inside of the wood (Fig. 41). There should be a margin of about $1\frac{1}{2}$ inches of tape on the sides and at least 3 inches on the ends, where the squeegee starts and stops and the ink is placed. Be sure that the tape on the inside of the screen extends $\frac{1}{4}$ to $\frac{1}{2}$ inch beyond the tape on the bottom, to avoid creating a buildup of tape in the margin. When such a buildup is allowed to occur, it can interfere with the action of the squeegee.

After taping has been completed, apply a coating of either shellac or lacquer to the taped areas on both sides of the screen. The coating should extend about $\frac{3}{8}$ inch onto the fabric itself. This helps seal the tape and prevent leakage of water and ink. (Lacquer thinner will dissolve lacquer, and alcohol will dissolve the shellac.)

A special tape available from screenprinting supply houses adheres with water and is lacquer resistant. It is much thicker than regular gummed tape, however, and this may present a problem in the printing process.

An alternative to taping the screen is to cover the wood and margins of the screen with epoxy resin. On the inside of the screen, where the fabric and inside edge of the wood meet, place enough epoxy to form a well. Epoxy is unaffected by the solvents and solutions used in normal printing and makes a very permanent sealing agent for the frame and margins of the screen when it is applied properly.

Devices for Raising the Screen

The screen must be raised after each stroke of the squeegee, so that the finished print can be removed and a new sheet of paper or section of fabric placed underneath. The simplest device for keeping the screen raised is a *drop stick,* a thin strip of wood about $\frac{3}{8}$ inch wide, $\frac{3}{4}$ inch high, and about 8 inches long. The drop stick is attached to one side of the frame so that it pivots freely. When the screen is lifted, the strip of wood drops down, propping the screen up at an angle (Fig. 42). This enables you to have both hands free to remove the paper and repeat the printing operation.

42. The drop stick device holds up the screen, leaving both hands free to prepare for the next print.

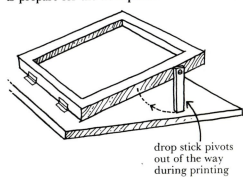

drop stick pivots out of the way during printing

43. The spring-loaded prop automatically lifts the screen when pressure from the squeegee is removed after each print.

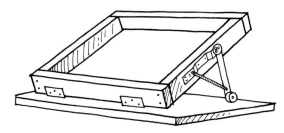

A spring-loaded *side kick* device can be clamped to the side of the screen frame to raise the screen automatically after printing. To print, press down on the squeegee and the screen will be lowered to the surface (Fig. 43).

Other lifting arrangements include the *counterbalance lift,* in which an arm extending back beyond the edge of the printing table is attached to the side of the frame. An adjustable weight that can be clamped at varying distances from the screen to regulate the lifting capacity is attached to the arm (Fig. 44). The *door spring lift* involves a raised support near the back of the frame. A door spring is attached to the top of the raised support at one end, while the other end is attached to the front of the screen frame. A *pulley lift* is convenient on large screens. It allows for the exact regulation of the lifting capacity in relation to the weight of the screen itself.

The Screenprinting Unit

A completely portable and very convenient screenprinting unit can be made by attaching the screen to a baseboard with hinges. The baseboard not only protects the screen, but also eliminates the need to find a flat surface for the printing surface (Figs. 42, 43). The

44. The counterbalance lift raises the screen by means of an adjustable weight. This arrangement was photographed at Fine Creations, Inc., New York.

baseboard should be made of $\frac{1}{2}$- or $\frac{3}{4}$-inch smooth and absolutely flat plywood or Novaply. Formica adhered to a piece of plywood with epoxy also makes an excellent baseboard.

The hinges for attaching the screen frame to the baseboard can be of several types. The most common is the brass door hinge, made in two parts and held together by a pin. If the baseboard is to be used for more than one frame, as in a multicolor print, the position of the hinges must be identical on each frame so that the frames will be in register. Special clamp hinges available from screenprinting supply houses can be either screwed into the baseboard or clamped onto one edge. The screen is held to the hinge by clamps. Screens can be changed without encountering difficulty when using the clamp-type hinges.

Blocks of wood should be placed on either side of the open screen area so that they just touch the frame when it is in the printing position. This will prevent any sideways movement of the screen due to looseness in the hinges and also will aid in close registration, particularly on large screens.

The Squeegee

The squeegee is the device that pulls the screenprinting ink across the surface of the screen, pushing it through the open areas onto the paper or cloth beneath it. It consists of a wooden or metal casing that holds a rubber or plastic blade. Different blade shapes are available for different kinds of screenprinting (Fig. 45). Because the blade is the most critical element of the squeegee, its condition and flexibility help determine the final results. It must be kept clean and adequately sharpened. Masking tape placed all around the squeegee where the blade and handle meet will greatly assist in cleaning after printing. The tape can be easily removed when changing colors and replaced with fresh tape.

For printing on flat objects, such as paper and cardboard, the square-edged blade is the one most commonly used. A square-edged blade with rounded corners is best to place heavy deposits of ink on any flat surface and to print fluorescent colors or light colors over dark. The single-sided bevel edge is used for printing on glass or name plates, and the double-sided bevel edge serves for printing on round or uneven surfaces, such as bottles or other containers. It is also convenient for printing fine detail on textiles. The round-edged squeegee blade is used mainly for textile printing. It allows for the necessary heavy deposits of ink. For ceramic printing, use a dou-bled-sided bevel edge with a flat point. The ceramic glazes are mixed with a vehicle, printed on decal paper, and then transferred to the ceramic ware and fired.

Squeegee casings and blades can be purchased as separate units or already assembled. The assembled squeegee and the individual blade are both sold by the inch. The squeegee should be at least an

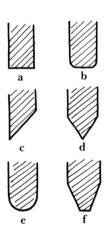

45. Various types of squeegee blades:
(a) square-edged,
(b) square-edged with rounded corners,
(c) single-sided bevel edge,
(d) double-sided bevel edge,
(e) round edge,
(f) double-sided bevel edge
with flat point.

Hardness of Squeegee Blades

Types of Blades	Durometer Readings
soft	40–45
medium	50–55
hard	60–65
extra hard	70–80

inch larger than the image on either side, and at the same time be 1 to 2 inches shorter than the inside dimensions of the frame. This will allow for free movement of the squeegee during the printing stroke. The well-equipped shop should have a good variety of squeegees of different lengths, for the smallest to the largest images. A one-hand squeegee with a handle attached in the center works well for small and medium-size images, since it frees the other hand for removing the prints and placing paper or cloth under the frame.

Squeegee Blade Composition

All squeegee blades are available in three basic degrees of hardness—soft, medium, and hard. For the vast majority of work on all types of surfaces, the medium blade is best. See the table above. Blades are made of several different types of materials, having different characteristics. Three common types are neoprene, rubber, and polyurethane.

Neoprene   A black neoprene blade can be used with all types of oil-base inks and all synthetic colors. It wears sooner than other blades, however, and requires more frequent sharpenings. Fine particles of the blade may show up occasionally in very light or transparent colors as the blade is worn down during printing.

Rubber   Rubber blades are actually composed of a synthetic rubber called *buna* and are a grayish-tan color. These blades have excellent resiliency and good wearing ability. They outlast neoprene blades and do not produce streaks. Rubber blades can be used with all oils, lacquers, and water-base colors. They resist lacquer thinners, alcohol, and other solvents.

Polyurethane   Polyurethane plastic, usually a transparent amber color, is the most durable of all blade materials. It requires less maintenance than any other material and remains sharp for longer periods of time, even with hard usage. The sharpness of the edge will produce a crisply defined image. It resists all solvents and is compatible with all printing inks.

Sharpening the Squeegee

A sharp squeegee is essential for clear and even printing. A simple sharpening device can be made by gluing strips of medium sandpaper or garnet paper onto a flat surface. Garnet paper is available at all screenprinting supply sources, in strips 6 inches wide and any length. Sheets of sandpaper can also be pieced together to make a sharpening device of any length. The sharpening device should be as long as the longest squeegee in the shop. To use it, hold the squeegee in a vertical position, with the flat part of the blade against the garnet paper or sandpaper, and saw the blade back and forth until the edges are sharp (Fig. 46). For large squeegees, two people—one at either end—perform this operation. Automatic sharpeners with motorized sanding devices will do the job in seconds. For a small shop, however, the expense of such a unit is rarely justified.

The One-Person Squeegee Unit

A one-person squeegee unit enables one person to print large images with relatively little effort (Fig. 47). The main part of the unit is a counterbalanced arm on which the squeegee is attached. After the angle of the squeegee has been adjusted to the best printing angle, pressure is applied to the single arm as the squeegee is pulled across the screen. The opposite side of the arm runs across a bar on bearings or rollers parallel to the direction in which the squeegee

46. Sharpen the squeegee blade by drawing it back and forth along a strip of garnet paper.

47. A one-person squeegee unit at Gemini G.E.L., Los Angeles.

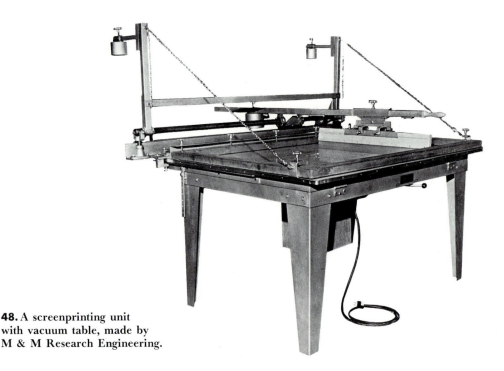

48. A screenprinting unit
with vacuum table, made by
M & M Research Engineering.

travels. These units are available for printing images ranging in size from 24 by 30 inches to over 5 by 10 feet. The one-person unit in combination with a vacuum table is ideal for both small and large print runs.

A vacuum table is a printing table with hundreds of small holes drilled into the surface. Suction is created when the vacuum is on, drawing air through the holes and holding paper firmly against the surface during printing. Once the paper has been printed, the vacuum is turned off so that the paper can be removed. A vacuum unit is essential for all critical registration (Fig. 48).

Drying Facilities

The drying arrangement for the finished prints is one of the most important aspects of screenprinting on paper. It should be considered well in advance of the actual printing. Screenprinting is a fast, efficient process, and it is important to provide for a way of stacking or racking the prints so that the printing can continue uninterrupted for the length of the run. A number of different drying arrangements can be devised, such as a clothesline arrangement, a metal or wooden drying rack, a rack device with clothespins, a fixed tray rack, or a strip rack (Figs. 49–51). The area in which both printing and drying take place should be well ventilated to enable the evaporating solvents to escape. In addition, the area should always be equipped with a large, explosion-proof fan.

After use, the ideal storage for the frame is a rack like that shown in Figure 52.

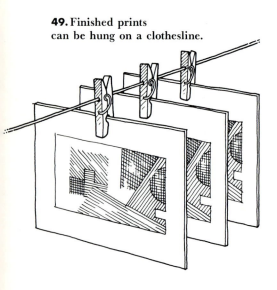

49. Finished prints
can be hung on a clothesline.

50. A screenprint
by Roy Lichtenstein is dried
in a hinged metal rack
at Styria Studios, New York.

51. Another drying device
uses clothespins nailed to a fixed rack
to hold the prints (a).
A fixed rack can also be constructed
to hold prints vertically
where space is not a consideration (b).

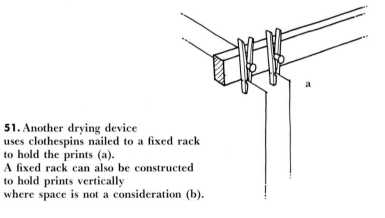

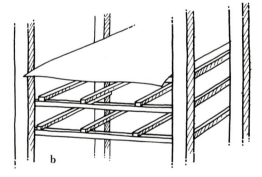

52. A storage rack for screens.

THREE

Chemicals and Solvents

In screenprinting, a knowledge of the function and properties of the various chemicals and solvents is indispensable. Because of the large number of solvents used, particularly in the cleaning-up procedures, it is important to know of the dangers that exist in both the toxicity of these materials and their volatility. Many solvents, in addition to being highly flammable, produce vapors that are extremely toxic.

Two of the most important considerations with all chemicals and solvents are proper storage facilities (Fig. 53) and proper ventilation. Fireproof solvent cans and metal storage cabinets that meet local fire ordinances are fairly standardized, and these ordinances should be complied with for maximum safety.

Health Hazards

Proper ventilation during all phases of screenprinting—from preparation through cleanup and print drying—is essential, so that the amount of solvent inhaled from the surrounding atmosphere is minimized. Over a period of years, as irritating substances get into the bloodstream through the lungs, the liver and kidneys can be damaged, since these organs attempt to detoxify and eliminate the harmful chemicals. Both red and white blood cells can be destroyed by chemical intrusion into the body's system. Chemicals like carbon monoxide and solvents such as toluol and benzol can reduce the cell count and cause oxygen starvation, which, in serious cases, can

53. A fireproof cabinet for storing chemicals.

permanently damage brain tissue. Side effects such as extreme weakness, palpitations, and anemia may be symptomatic of excessive exposure to unhealthy conditions. Pulmonary problems caused by toxic chemicals of various kinds are often mistaken for influenza or bronchial congestion.

Although it might take years of heavy exposure to many solvents or chemicals to produce some of the serious conditions described above, there is no doubt that many individuals whose systems have an extremely low tolerance for toxic substances could be affected in a relatively short period of time. Cumulative effects may also be experienced by persons who are heavy smokers or who live in heavily industrialized areas.

Some solvents and chemicals, in addition to presenting a hazard by inhalation, can create problems in contact. This can lead to chronic skin problems, including dermatitis and severe allergic reactions. In order to avoid direct contact with any acid, alkali, or solvent, always wear rubber or plastic gloves.

Following is a listing of the chemicals and solvents common in screenprinting, their uses and characteristics, and how they can be handled safely.

Acids

Acetic Acid

Acetic acid in highly concentrated form (99½ percent) is called *glacial acetic acid.* It has a highly pungent odor and can cause severe burns if contact is made with the skin. When used in screenprinting, it is diluted to a solution of about 5 percent acid to 95 percent water. This is about the strength of vinegar, which is itself a diluted form of acetic acid and can be used whenever this acid is needed.

The dilute acetic-and-water solution serves to neutralize the screen after cleaning with bleach or chlorine-activated cleaning powders. It also destroys the enzymes in some cleaners that remove gelatin-based emulsions from the screen. Some water-soluble handcut stencils are best adhered to the screen with a dilute acetic acid and isopropyl alcohol mixture. In its dilute form or as vinegar, acetic acid poses no great hazard.

Alkalies

Bleach (Sodium Hypochlorite)

Sodium hypochlorite is used to remove direct photographic emulsions from the screen. It is identical to the household variety of laundry bleach. At full strength it removes direct photo emulsions, but it must be applied only to synthetic (nylon, polyester) fabrics, for it destroys silk and other organic material. Sodium hypochlorite is neutralized by dilute acetic acid. Always wear rubber gloves when handling this bleach and take care not to splash it about or to get it into your eyes.

Hydrogen Peroxide

Hydrogen peroxide, as a weak 3-percent solution, is used for antiseptic purposes and is available in any drugstore. A 6-percent solution of this alkali, used as a developer for many presensitized photo stencil films, can be obtained from screen supply sources. In this mild form, hydrogen peroxide can be used safely with gloves, although contact with the eyes should be avoided. To prevent skin sensitization, wash areas of skin contact with soap and water.

Ammonia

At times, a small quantity of ammonia is added to potassium or ammonium bichromate sensitizing solutions to increase their sensitizing properties. Always wear gloves when using ammonia, and ensure that the area is well ventilated, because ammonia vapors are a strong irritant to the eyes, nose, and lungs.

Ink Solvents
and Cleaning Solvents

Mineral Spirits (Paint Thinner)

Mineral spirits is the most commonly used substance for diluting oil-base inks and for cleaning up. This inexpensive solvent is available at most hardware stores. It has a high flash point and does not become dangerously volatile except above 100°F. However, it will ignite at normal temperatures if exposed to an open flame. When using mineral spirits for cleaning, wear gloves and keep the area well ventilated. Unlike turpentine, which is a product of wood fermentation and distillation, mineral spirits is petroleum based.

Kerosene

A petroleum-base solvent, kerosene has a high flash point similar to that of mineral spirits. It is an inexpensive solvent and often is employed to clean the screen of normal solvent-base poster inks. Because of its slow drying characteristics, small quantities of it are used as a retarder for the poster inks. Kerosene is flammable and should not be used near an open flame, a lighted cigarette, or where there is danger of sparks. Place rags used with kerosene in metal fireproof containers and dispose of rags daily to preclude the possibility of spontaneous combustion.

Lacquer Thinner

All lacquer thinners are a mixture of various solvents such as toluol, acetone, alcohol, and xylol. The ingredients vary according to use. Special thinners are recommended for lacquer stencil adhesion because they evaporate without leaving a residual film. Common lacquer thinner, of the type available in hardware stores, is helpful in cleaning stubborn ink from screens, and in dissolving lacquer blockout and lacquer stencil film. This solvent is also used as a thinner for lacquer-base inks as well as a cleaning solvent for acrylic inks. All lacquer thinners are extremely volatile and have a relatively low flash point, making them highly flammable. Good ventilation is important. When cleaning screens with lacquer thinner, set up a fan to direct the vapors away from you. The strong odor of lacquer thinner provides, to some degree, a measurement of the concentration of solvent in any enclosed space.

Acetone

Acetone, a highly aromatic and volatile solvent, is the main ingredient of lacquer thinners. It will dissolve stubborn ink spots, lacquer blockout, or film from the screen. Because it is extremely flammable, it should be used with caution and kept in fireproof metal containers and cabinets. Acetone vapors and alcohol vapors, in moderate concentrations, are among the least toxic of the strong solvents; however, good ventilation is advised.

Alcohol

A thinner and solvent for shellac, alcohol is also a solvent for epoxy resin before hardening takes place.

All alcohols used in screenprinting are denatured, which means that a chemical substance is added to the pure alcohol, making it both noxious and poisonous for human consumption. This added substance cannot be isolated from the pure alcohol either by distillation, filtration, or other means.

Isopropyl alcohol (rubbing alcohol), found in all drugstores, is available usually in two concentrations, 70 percent and 99 percent. It is useful for all techniques but is more expensive than the alcohol solvent sold in hardware stores.

Methyl alcohol (wood alcohol), distilled from wood pulp fermentation, is applicable for all techniques which require alcohol. Adequate ventilation is necessary, for it is a highly toxic substance.

Ethyl alcohol (ethanol) is made from distilling various grains and vegetables, including corn, potatoes, and rye. As a solvent, it is available only in a crude, denatured form. Anhydrous alcohol is a completely water-free alcohol of the methy-ethyl type.

Benzine (V.M. & P. Naphtha)

Benzine is a refined petroleum distillate similar to gasoline. It is highly flammable and evaporates quickly, leaving no residue or trace elements. With a flash point under 73°F, benzine vapors can unite with oxygen to form an explosive mixture. However, it is safe to use with good ventilation. (Benzine should not be confused with *benzene,* which contains benzol, a dangerous solvent that can have a cumulative and chronic poisoning effect on bone marrow, leading to loss of red or white blood cells.)

Turpentine

Several kinds of turpentine are available from either screen supply houses or hardware stores. All types are excellent for cleaning screens. The most common types are wood sulphite turpentine, steam distilled, and gum turpentine. Turpentine leaves behind a slight residue of resinous material after evaporation. However, this can be removed with any of the more volatile solvents, such as acetone, lacquer thinner, or benzine. Turpentine can cause allergic reactions in some people, and gloves should be worn for cleaning.

Lithotine

As a turpentine substitute, lithotine exhibits all the effective qualities of turpentine but without the allergic effects of the natural product. It is composed primarily of petroleum-base mineral spirits or benzine with small amounts of pine oil, castor oil, and ester gum.

Other turpentine substitutes such as Nankee ST100 are available from screen supply sources.

Methyl Chloride

Methyl chloride is a highly volatile solvent which, when combined with alcohol, will thin some types of water-soluble blockout to speed drying. Use it only for this purpose and with good ventilation.

Xylol and Toluol

Both xylol and toluol are highly volatile solvents often combined in some lacquer thinners. They are effective in cleaning screens, though good ventilation is required during the process.

Ethylene Dichloride

Similar to methyl chloride, ethylene dichloride is also used with that solvent to dilute some water-soluble blockout solutions. It should be used only with good ventilation.

Cellosolve (Ethylene Glucol Monoethyl Ether)
Cellosolve Acetate

Cellosolve and cellosolve acetate are similar slow-acting solvents occasionally recommended for cleaning tough-to-remove dried ink from screens. Screens, brushes, and tools can be soaked overnight to soften lacquer and other inks. Cellosolve acetate, used for magazine transfers in lithography, can also transfer magazine images to vellum for making positives in photo screenprinting. Careful handling of these solvents in well-ventilated areas must be observed.

Methyl Cellosolve Acetate
(Ethylene Glycol Monomethyl Ether Acetate)

Methyl cellosolve acetate, although similar to the preceding two cellosolve solvents, is considerably more dangerous to use. This solvent is extremely toxic and should not be used.

Other Chemical Substances
Used in Screenprinting

Polyvinyl Acetate
Polyvinyl Alcohol

These two ingredients, polyvinyl acetate and polyvinyl alcohol, are usually found together in water-base emulsions used for direct photo applications. When mixed with either an ammonium or potassium bichromate solution, this substance becomes light sensitive and hardens upon exposure. It has a long shelf life prior to sensitization.

Ammonium Bichromate
Potassium Bichromate

Ammonium bichromate and potassium bichromate, two light-sensitive salts, are mixed with water, and used with direct photo emulsions. Available in dry crystalline form, they mix easily with water. Both of these salts are brilliant orange in color. When mixed in similar concentrations, ammonium bichromate produces an emulsion in approximately half the time as the potassium bichromate, thus requiring about 50 percent less exposure time. They produce no fumes and are not flammable. However, both are poisonous and can cause severe skin reactions. Always wear rubber gloves when using either, and wash your hands with soap and water after contact.

Trisodium Phosphate

Trisodium phosphate is a strong degreasing agent used for preparing screen mesh for photo emulsions. It is obtainable from screen supply sources as Mesh Prep or Screen Prep. Add 1 tablespoon of trisodium phosphate to 1 quart of water. Place this solution on the screen, and scrub on both sides with a cloth or brush. Rinse the screen thoroughly with water. After rinsing, apply a mild solution of acetic acid and water on the screen to complete the degreasing operation. Then thoroughly rinse the screen and dry it.

FOUR

Stencil-Making Techniques

In screenprinting, the basis for any image is the substance or material used to fill openings in the screen corresponding to non-printing areas. Many ordinary substances—such as water-soluble glue, lacquer, and shellac—can be applied directly to the fabric on all nonprinting areas to form the *blockout*. This is perhaps the simplest means of making a stencil, and it is well suited for bold images in which detail and perfect edges are not required.

In a more positive method of working, two substances whose solvents are incompatible can be used in making the stencil. For example, an image can be created directly on the fabric with a water-soluble glue. When this has dried, a thin coating of lacquer is applied over the entire screen. When the lacquer in turn has dried, the glue is dissolved with water, lifting the lacquer on top of it and leaving the screen open in the positive, image areas. The lacquer remaining on the screen blocks the passage of ink in the nonprinting areas. A wide variety of substances can serve in similar ways to create images. It is important, therefore, to understand the nature of stencil-making materials and their solvents. In the following techniques, these materials will be needed:

- o glue (Lepages Original or Franklin Hide Glue)
- o shellac
- o denatured or anhydrous alcohol
- o lacquer blockout

o water-soluble blockout
o lithographic crayon or tusche
o rubber cement
o lacquer thinner
o turpentine, lithotine, or kerosene
o paint thinner
o phosphoric, hydrochloric, or glacial acetic acid
o glycerine
o Maskoid or E-Z Liquid Frisket
o tracing paper, layout paper, or bond paper
o clean rags, sponges, and newspaper
o scoop coater

Characteristics of Basic Blockout Solutions

Glue   Lepages Original Glue and Franklin Hide Glue are two of the best kinds of glue to use for screenprinting. Both are quite viscous and can be thinned with water up to a 50 percent solution for easier application to the screen. This is necessary especially when the glue is used as a coating over the entire screen. Two thinned coats of solution applied separately are better than one heavy coat in this case.

Since glue is transparent, the addition of a small amount of watercolor or poster color will help to make it visible on the screen. Liquid food coloring, which does not contain pigments, is also excellent and produces a smooth, flowing blockout. The addition of 2 to 4 percent glycerine will help to make the glue more flexible and easier to work with.

Shellac   Both orange shellac and white shellac are suitable for the stencil-making process. *Five-pound cut shellac* is preferable, since it has a heavy consistency and will go further. It can be thinned when necessary with common denatured or anhydrous alcohol.

Lacquer Blockout   A tough, flexible lacquer called *lacquer block-out* can be used as a screen filler and for touching up handcut lacquer film and photo stencils. It works with all oil-, enamel-, cellulose-, and water-base inks but cannot be used with lacquer or vinyl inks.

Water-Soluble Blockout   *Water-soluble blockout* can serve in place of glue for any of the screenprinting techniques discussed subsequently. This substance creates a strong, flexible film that can produce hundreds of impressions and can be seen and retouched easily because of its color. It washes out of the screen with warm or cold water, but cannot be used with a water-base ink because the

Drawing Materials, Screen Fillers, and their Solvents

Substance	Solvent
glue (Lepages Original Glue, Franklin Hide Glue) **and water-soluble blockout**	water
shellac (white or orange)	alcohol, acetone (dissolves slowly in lacquer thinner)
lacquer blockout	lacquer thinner, acetone
litho crayon, tusche	turpentine, lithotine, kerosene, paint thinner, lacquer thinner, acetone, benzine, mineral spirits
rubber cement, Maskoid	rubber cement thinner (also can be removed from the screen with a rubber cement eraser)

blockout will be dissolved. Water-soluble blockout is good for oil-base inks, lacquers, enamels, and any textile inks that do not contain water. See the table above.

Glue-Shellac Method

A stencil-making technique that uses glue and shellac can create a positive image. A guide drawing can be placed beneath the screen first to make a more accurate stencil. The glue, which can be made more visible with watercolor paint or poster paint, is then applied directly to the image areas (Fig. 54). When it is dry, the entire surface is covered with a thin coat of shellac, applied with a small squeegee or a piece of cardboard (Fig. 55). In applying shellac, be careful not to leave too much on the image areas, or otherwise it will

below left:
54. Michelle Juristo
drawing on the screen with tinted glue.

below right:
55. Applying shellac with cardboard.

be difficult to wash out the glue. Once the shellac has dried, wash out the glue with a spray of cold water, and check the screen for pinholes against a light source. Touch up if necessary by applying shellac over the holes. Water-soluble blockout can be used in place of glue for this method. It has the advantage of being easier to see on the screen and is less brittle than glue when dry. When this method is used on silk fabric, it may be difficult to remove the shellac from the silk after printing. Alcohol alone does not always work, and it may be necessary to alternate alcohol with acetone and lacquer thinner to ensure a clean screen.

Glue-Lacquer Method

In the glue-lacquer method, as in the glue-shellac method, the positive image is drawn onto the screen with glue. Again, a drawing can be placed underneath to serve as a guide for the work, or a pencil drawing can be made directly on the screen. Watercolor or poster paint can also be added to the glue. After the completed glue image has dried, apply a thin, even coating of lacquer or lacquer blockout over the screen with a small squeegee or a piece of cardboard. Once the lacquer coating has dried, wash the glue from the screen with warm water. The image areas can be cleaned further by rubbing them lightly with a sponge and water to remove both the glue and the lacquer over the glue.

   This method can also be reversed by using lacquer blockout as the positive drawing medium and glue as the overall filler. Remove the lacquer from the screen with lacquer thinner; the glue will remain on the screen in the nonimage areas. All types of inks except water-base inks can be used with this method.

Tusche-Glue Method

The use of liquid tusche to form the stencil allows for painterly effects that imitate the fluidity and immediacy of direct brushwork. Screens of silk or multifilament polyester work best for this technique. The screen must be clean of any soap, sizing, or grease.

56. Harry Hurwitz applying liquid Toosh (a superior brand of tusche) for the tusche-glue technique.

57. Applying glue to the image
with a piece of mat board.

58. Washing the Toosh
from the screen with kerosene.

Make a pencil drawing directly on the screen to serve as a guide
for the tusche drawing. Shake the bottled tusche well, and pour it
into a shallow dish. It should be about the consistency of heavy
cream. Then apply the tusche directly to the top of the screen with
a brush, so that the image will read correctly when the screen is in
the printing position (Fig. 56). Allow the tusche to dry, then check
the screen by holding it up to the light. Parts of the image that are
to print as solid areas should be completely opaque. If necessary,
touch up with additional tusche. Once the tusche has dried, the
screen is ready for the application of the glue mixture.

The glue mixture, which serves as the blockout, consists of:

4 ounces Lepages Original Glue or Franklin Hide Glue
2½ ounces water
5–15 drops acid (phosphoric, hydrochloric, or glacial acetic)
10 drops glycerine

Apply this mixture over the top surface of the entire screen with
a small squeegee or a piece of cardboard. Since the mixture is thin,
apply two light coats. If small pinholes of light appear, touch them
up afterwards. The glue should be applied on the same side of the
screen as the tusche, or it will seal the tusche in and prevent
complete washout (Fig. 57).

When the glue has dried, wash the tusche out with kerosene,
working on the bottom side of the screen (Fig. 58). In this way, the
tusche will dissolve readily and lift off any glue that has adhered to

59. A proof of the finished print.
The image retains
all of the original brushwork.

it. Scrub the screen lightly with a nylon brush to help dislodge particles of tusche from the edges of the image and to bring out the subtle brushstroke effects achieved by this technique (Fig. 59).

Because tusche is a mixture of wax, shellac, soap, and black pigment, it is soluble in water and in petroleum solvents such as kerosene, turpentine, mineral spirits, and lacquer thinner. Glue thinned with water might therefore begin to dissolve the tusche when it is applied over it. This is the reason for the presence of acid in the glue solution. The acid reacts with the tusche and hardens it, still leaving it vulnerable to kerosene or other solvents. A small percentage of glycerine in the glue makes it more flexible and less brittle. Coloring matter, such as watercolor or gouache, can make the mixture more visible.

Water-soluble blockout can substitute for glue. The formula should be modified as follows:

4 ounces water-soluble blockout
3 ounces water
5 drops acid (phosphoric, hydrochloric, or glacial acetic)

Just before printing check the screen for pinholes again. Completely white areas and margins can be given an additional coat of glue or blockout solution to make the stencil more ink-resistant.

Litho Crayon-Glue Method

The litho crayon-glue method is technically the same as the tusche-glue method, except that litho crayons (or rubbing ink) are

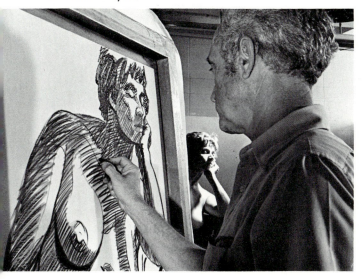

60. Harrison Covington working
directly on the screen
with litho crayon.

61. After coating the drawing side
of the screen, wash out
the crayon image with lithotine.

used in place of, or in combination with, tusche (Fig. 60). This
method provides another positive means of working on the screen,
with results similar in appearance to a crayon drawing.

Any of the three grades of rubbing ink (soft, medium, and hard)
will perform well, although with litho crayons the softest grades
(Nos. 00, 0, 1, 2, and 3) are best. When using litho crayon, make the
drawing stronger than the final image is to be, to compensate for the
slight visual loss that results in this process. A guide drawing or
sketch can be placed directly under the screen. Both the drawing
and the screen should be held firmly so that they do not shift. The
technique of placing the screen over textured objects or surfaces and
rubbing it with litho crayon (as if you were making a stone rubbing)
affords an almost inexhaustible source for new effects.

When the image is complete, treat the stencil in the same
manner as the tusche stencil, applying the glue or blockout on
the drawing side of the screen, then washing out the crayon image
with lithotine (Fig. 61).

Other Solutions
for Making Stencils

Maskoid and E-Z Liquid Frisket are opaque latex solutions that
congeal when dry. They can be applied directly to the screen with a
brush or other drawing instrument and are fluid enough to be used
in a ruling pen for fine linear work. When the screen is dry, glue or
water-soluble blockout is applied over the entire screen on one side
only, as in the preceding methods, in two (or possibly three) thin
coats. Let the screen dry thoroughly, then remove the Maskoid or
E-Z Frisket by rubbing with a rubber cement eraser.

62. Oshaweetuk.
Four Musk Oxen. 1959.
Eskimo stencil print,
image $5\frac{1}{8} \times 17''$ (13 × 42 cm).
Brooklyn Museum, New York.

The Paper Stencil

Making a stencil with paper is one of the easiest methods to undertake, and although the stencil will not withstand prolonged printing, many good impressions can be produced this way. The technique is best suited for large, bold images.

The deposit of ink depends on the thickness of the paper used. The heavier the paper, the heavier the deposit of ink will be—particularly at the edges of the image, which tend to be sharply defined. Tracing paper, layout paper, and even ordinary bond paper can be used for cutting the stencil. Cut openings in the paper to represent the image, and place the cutout underneath the screen. The paper should extend as far as the frame, so that ink does not seep beyond the stencil area. The stencil will adhere to the screen with the first pass of the squeegee. The outer edges can be taped to the frame; floating parts of the image can be held in place with a spot of glue.

Disadvantages of this method are that it is difficult to make corrections once printing has begun, and each stencil can be used with only one color. Clean-up is simplified greatly, however. Peel the stencil paper away from the screen and clean the ink from the screen with a solvent, rags, and newspapers.

Pochoir

The simplicity of the *pochoir* technique often causes it to be underrated as a means for adding color or new images to a print (Pl. 6, p. 60). *Pochoir* is a stencil technique in which shapes are cut out of a thin plastic such as Mylar or acetate, thin brass or copper plates, or oiled stencil paper. The color is dabbed onto the print through the opening with a stencil brush or sometimes with a roller. A fairly soft roller and thin stencil will produce the sharpest possible image.

Extremely fine results are possible with this technique (Fig. 62), and the consistency in quality for any size edition can be maintained very accurately, both for heavy deposits of ink and for thin transparencies of color.

Plate 5. Richard Anuszkiewicz. *Blue to Red Portal.* 1977.
Screenprint on Masonite, 7 × 4′ (2.1 × 1.2 m).
Courtesy Editions Lassiter-Meisel, New York.

Plate 6. Henri Matisse. *The Burial of Pierrot,* Plate VIII from *Jazz.* 1947. Pochoir, 16¼ × 25⅛″ (41 × 63 cm). The Grunewald Center for Graphic Arts, University of California, Los Angeles.

Lacquer Stencil Film

Handcut lacquer stencil film creates sharp, hard-edged images. It is used commercially for large type and images, as well as for fine art applications in which bold, solid areas or crisp detail are necessary. Designs that are cut into stencil film can be infinitely more detailed than those made with a paper stencil, and they are strong enough to yield thousands of impressions. The required materials for making a stencil from lacquer film are:

- ○ lacquer film
- ○ a small stencil knife or X-acto knife with a pointed blade
- ○ lacquer adhering liquid
- ○ clean, soft rags or cloths
- ○ a well-prepared screen

Lacquer stencil film consists of a thin sheet of lacquer adhered to a paper or plastic backing. It is available in rolls 36, 40, or 44 inches wide, and up to 300 inches long. The lacquer film is cut with a sharp pointed knife and peeled away from the backing. The areas that are removed are those that will print. The film remaining on the backing paper is adhered to the screen, and then its backing is removed. Lacquer stencil film can be used with all inks, except those that are lacquer or vinyl based.

Cutting the Film

Lacquer film comes in a number of different colors, all transparent so that a drawing can be placed underneath to guide the cutting. The lacquer (emulsion) side should be up. The design is cut piece by piece, with the knife held in a vertical position (Fig. 63), and the lacquer film is peeled away from the backing sheet by using the

63. Lacquer stencil film can be taped to a light table during the cutting. Note the angle of the knife.

64. Lift the film with the point of the knife.

point of the knife (Fig. 64). Exert enough pressure on the knife to cut through the film only, and not through the paper or plastic backing. It takes some practice to find the proper touch.

A special cutting knife is made by the Ulano Company expressly for stencil cutting. It has a swivel blade of surgical steel mounted in a ball-bearing socket, making it ideal for cutting both intricate, curved shapes and large, geometric images. The blade can be made stable by tightening a knob on the handle. Other good and less expensive knives are available, some with swivel blades and some without. The X-acto knife is a good, all-purpose knife for cutting paper stencils and film stencils. Special compass cutters are also available for cutting circles. There are bicutters with twin blades that cut parallel lines simultaneously. Some bicutters are adjustable and can cut lines of varying widths. Film line cutters are used for cutting fine lines with a single stroke. These come in a set of three tools that cut and peel the film simultaneously in differing widths.

Adhering the Film to the Screen

Good adhesion of the film to the screen fabric depends upon having a clean, properly prepared screen. There should be no trace of oil, grease, sizing, or any other foreign material on its surface. Monofilament fabric screens, especially if they are new, should be given a "tooth" to ensure better adhesion of the film to the fabric. The adhering process is as follows:

1. Make sure the film has been removed from all image areas. Set the remaining film on a smooth, flat table with the lacquer side up, and place a few small tabs of masking tape on each corner, so that as the screen is lowered, the film will be held lightly to the bottom. Lower the screen to the film. A piece of cardboard

or Masonite placed under the film will raise it slightly from the table, allowing more pressure to be applied.

2. Pour enough lacquer adhering liquid on a cotton rag to make it thoroughly wet, but not dripping. Working outward from the center, apply the liquid to the screen, and wipe the area immediately with a dry pad, rubbing with light but even pressure to push the softened stencil into the fabric (Fig. 65). The areas that have adhered well will begin to appear darker. Work on only a small area at a time, and do not allow the adhering liquid to remain on the film, for it could dissolve the film.

3. When the film appears to be adhered evenly without bubbles or light spots, allow it to dry for 15 or 20 minutes. A fan will speed up the drying. When the film has dried, remove the tabs of masking tape from the corners, and peel off the backing sheet slowly, starting from a corner (Fig. 66). If pieces of film begin to lift off with the backing sheet, reapply them with the solvent and allow another, longer period for drying.

left: 65. Adhere the film
to the screen with adhering liquid,
using light, even pressure.

above: 66. Starting from a corner,
carefully peel the backing
away from the adhered film.

Lacquer Stencil Film **63**

67. Blockout solution is applied
to the margins before printing.

68. A proof of the complete image.

4. Check the screen against the light, and touch up any pinhole
    spots with lacquer blockout solution and a brush on both the top
    and the bottom of the screen. Use blockout solution for the
    margins beyond the edges of the film as well (Fig. 67). The
    screen is now ready for printing (Fig. 68).

Water-Soluble Film

Water-soluble film, such as Ulano Aquafilm, is similar in appearance to lacquer film. It is unaffected by lacquer-, oil-, vinyl-, and petroleum-base solvents and inks, but can be softened and dissolved by water and by any solutions containing water. Water-soluble film should be cut in the same way as lacquer film; again cut through the emulsion only and not the backing.

Aquafilm is adhered to the screen in a slightly different manner than lacquer film. The adhering liquid recommended by the manufacturer is:

1 part isopropyl alcohol (90 percent)
2 parts acetic acid and water (5 percent acidity)

Ordinary white vinegar can take the place of acetic acid. Another formula calls for 3 parts water instead of acetic acid or vinegar.

To adhere the water-soluble film, wet a piece of cloth with adhering solution, and apply it generously to the top of the screen, working on only a small area at a time. Blot quickly with clean newsprint, Kim-wipes, or tissues, pressing firmly on the surface. Pressure helps to push the softened film into the screen fabric. The areas that have adhered well will appear darker. Continue to apply adhering liquid, blotting it immediately afterwards, until the entire film appears firmly attached to the screen. Allow 45 to 60 minutes for the film to dry; more in humid conditions.

When the film is dry, peel off the backing sheet carefully, and touch up any pinholes or imperfections, as well as all marginal areas of the screen up to the frame, with water-soluble blockout on both sides. This will ensure clean margins.

FIVE

Photographic Techniques

The Process Camera

The process camera, or "copy" camera, is one of the mainstays of the photographic print workshop and represents a considerable investment. It is basically similar to any other camera and is governed by the same general principles. Process cameras vary greatly in size, ranging from one that will take a 16-by-20-inch sheet of film to one that will take a 48-by-72-inch sheet. The most common size, for a 20-by-24-inch sheet, occupies a space about 12 feet long, from the extension of the copy board to the screen (Fig. 69).

Illumination is provided by carbon arc lamps, quartz iodine, pulsed zenon, or in some cases, by photoflood lamps. Most process cameras are horizontal and mounted on the floor, although many of the very large format cameras are suspended from an overhead rack. Vertical cameras have gained a considerable amount of popularity, mainly because of their space-saving design.

The basic camera has three main units: the copy board, the lens, and the focusing screen and film-holding device. The copy board holds the material to be photographed by means of a suction device, or under glass in a pressure frame. The axis of the lens is maintained at right angles to the copy board and to the ground glass focusing area. Provision is made at the back of the camera for replacing the focal plane of the ground glass with a piece of film and for holding halftone screens. Both the copy board and the lens can move along a track to change the relationships among film, lens, and copy, thus enlarging or reducing the focused image.

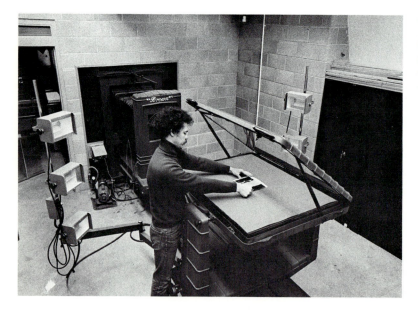

69. A process camera photographed at York University, Toronto. When the image has been positioned on the copy board, the board is tilted to a vertical position to face the lens of the camera. The lamps on the left are quartz iodine lamps.

The Photographic Negative

The most commonly used film for photolithography or photoengraving is a high-contrast *orthochromatic* film. This film is not sensitive to red light, so that a red light, such as Kodak Safelight Filter, Wratten Series 1A, can be used in the darkroom without danger to the film. Orthochromatic films, when used in combination with a prescribed developer, will produce negatives that are black and white only, without intermediate tonalities. In this respect they match the characteristics of the sensitized screen.

By comparison, films such as those used for snapshot photography are *panchromatic*—that is, sensitive to all colors. Negatives produced with this type of film are called *continuous tone negatives,* and have a full range of tonalities. When exposed onto sensitized paper and developed, they will produce the full-value photographic positive with which we are all familiar.

Line and Halftone Photography

A *line shot* is a photograph taken on orthochromatic film directly in the camera, without the use of a *halftone screen.* Line shots are generally used for type copy, linear work, and nontonal images. If an ordinary photograph, which has a continuous range of tonalities, were photographed as a line shot, the image would be reduced to stark black and white without intermediate tonalities.

In *halftone* photography, by comparison, tonal gradations in the image are simulated by placing a special contact (magenta) screen or glass halftone screen over the film before exposure. The screen is a grid of opaque vertical and horizontal lines that break up the tonalities of the image into dots on the film. Each minute opening in the grid creates a larger or smaller dot on the film, depending on whether more or less light is admitted. The total effect is of a continuous range of tonalities.

The screens themselves are calibrated by the number of lines per inch. Two of the most common sizes for magazine or brochure work have 120 or 133 lines per inch. Newspaper halftones have about 85 lines per inch, while some specialty work on coated paper might use a screen as fine as 400. For hand screening, a screen of about 133 lines per inch is usually the finest that can be printed.

Some other types of screens used to create halftones are the mezzotint screen, the elliptical dot screen, the parallel line screen, and the circular line screen. Each one can be used to break up the tonal scale of the original image into a regular or irregular pattern of dots or lines. Three of these are compared with a line shot below in Figure 70.

Exposures for Line and Halftone Photography

Since the sensitivity of different films varies, it is best to make test exposures according to each manufacturer's specifications. Kodak, for example, suggests a 10-second exposure at f/32 for same-size (1-to-1) line reproduction with Kodalith Ortho Film type 3; and when using a contact screen, the exposure should be 8 to 10 times longer. The greatest definition and resolution of most graphic-art lenses is found midway between the widest and the smallest apertures; f/16, f/22, or f/32 are therefore the apertures most commonly used whenever detailed work is to be reproduced. The light source is directed toward the copy from two sides at an angle of approximately 45 degrees, so that light is reflected away from the lens. This prevents "hot spots" on the image, which are caused by light bouncing back through the lens.

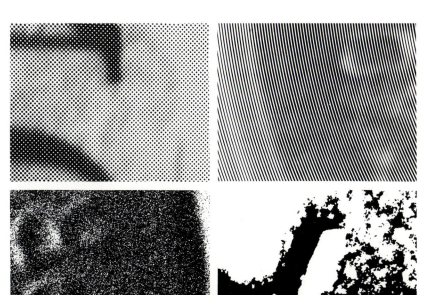

70. Top left, halftone dot screen; top right, halftone circular line screen; bottom left, mezzotint screen; bottom right, line shot (made without a screen).

Most contemporary workshops are equipped with facilities for using photographic images in etching, screenprinting, and lithographic techniques. The popularity of this manner of creating images has grown considerably in the last decade (Fig. 71). Photographic techniques need not be costly, for a great deal can be accomplished with a minimum of equipment. If you plan to employ photographic means to make your stencil, you will need all or some of the following materials:

○ photographic positive or handmade positive
○ Azoclean, Nylon Mesh Prep, Silk Mesh Prep, or powdered cleanser
○ stiff nylon scrub brush
○ acetic acid or vinegar (optional)
○ direct screen emulsion (diazo compound or ammonium bichromate)
○ presensitized film and developer
○ scoop coater
○ ultraviolet light source (carbon arc lamp, pulsed zenon, fluorescent light, or black light)
○ sheet of clear glass
○ water-soluble blockout, glue, or Kodak Red Photo Opaque
○ newsprint
○ vacuum table

The basis of all screen photographic processes is the *positive,* such as a photographic positive image or a hand-drawn, opaque image on transparent acetate (or other translucent material). This positive is placed either on a special sensitized film or against a screen coated with sensitized emulsion. Wherever light travels through the positive, the sensitized coating hardens, while the unexposed areas dissolve and become the open, printing areas.

There are two basic techniques: the *direct screen emulsion technique,* in which a light-sensitive coating is applied directly to the screen fabric; and the *indirect film technique,* in which a separate sensitized sheet of gelatinized film on a plastic support is adhered to the screen after being exposed and developed.

In order for the photo emulsion to adhere completely to the screen, the screen must be thoroughly clean and free of any foreign matter. Grease, ink, and other substances must be removed. Commercial preparations are excellent. These include Azoclean, a degreasing concentrate; Nylon Mesh Prep, which cleans and roughens nylon and monofilament polyester; and Silk Mesh Prep, for silk and multifilament polyester. Commercial household cleaning powders are also effective. All of these preparations are scrubbed on both sides of the screen with a stiff nylon brush and some warm water. A 5-percent solution of acetic acid or vinegar can be poured over the screen to neutralize any traces of chlorine from household cleaners.

71. Andy Warhol. *Vote McGovern.*
1972. Screenprint, 42″ (105 cm) square.
Courtesy Gemini G.E.L., Los Angeles.

The screen should always be rinsed thoroughly with clean, hot water after scrubbing, and be allowed to dry. Special attention should be given to cleaning and rinsing procedures when using multifilament fabrics, since particles of cleanser or detergent can remain lodged in the strands of the fabric.

The Direct Screen Emulsion Technique

Screen Fabrics

Monofilament polyester and nylon are ideal for use with direct photo emulsions. Special "anti-halo" fabrics designed for this purpose are dyed yellow or orange to prevent light from passing through the fabric at the edges of the image. Thus, no ragged edges are formed during exposure.

Although multifilament polyester can be used for direct emulsion work, monofilament nylon and polyester are preferred, because they are easier to clean. Monofilament fabrics also have a high percentage of open area, and ink flows freely through the strands of fabric. The most versatile fabrics for photo emulsion work have thread counts of 175 to 285. Since the photo emulsion surrounds the fabric, adhesion is excellent for long runs.

Solutions

Direct photo emulsions have been improved continually in the past decade. They are convenient, simple to apply, and easy to remove from the screen once the printing has been completed. Although they are more common in the commercial field, they have many artistic applications, both for photographic images and for direct drawing techniques. When used in combination with the "anti-halo" nylon or monofilament polyester, they make possible exquisite detail and sharpness. Ironically, it is possible to achieve even greater sharpness and more accurately rendered detail with a brush or an airbrush on translucent Mylar or acetate, than with tusche or litho crayon applied directly to the screen. There is little doubt that, as familiarity with direct photo emulsions grows and their exciting creative possibilities are realized, they will replace many older, less efficient techniques.

There are two types of direct screen emulsions. In one, the sensitizing base is a diazo compound; in the other direct screen emulsion, it is ammonium bichromate.

Diazo-Sensitized Photo Emulsion The diazo sensitizing compound is the newest sensitizer to come onto the market. Although it requires a longer exposure time, it is superior to the bichromate emulsion in many ways. The diazo emulsion screen produces images that are slightly sharper, cleaner, and less affected by light bounce or the "halo" sometimes associated with bichromate emulsions. Screens treated with this emulsion can be stored for more than three months without *dark reaction,* change in exposure, or loss of detail. Dark reaction is the hardening of film stored for long periods in the dark, in which the emulsion becomes insoluble.

There are a number of manufacturers who make basically the same product. Although there are slight differences, the results should be equally good and consistent if the manufacturers' specifications are followed carefully.

The Naz-Dar Company makes a product called Encosol-1. This consists of the liquid emulsion, the diazo sensitizer, and a blue dye concentrate, all of which come in separate containers. The sensitizer and emulsion form the basic transparent coating. The dye is added to allow close visual inspection at all stages of the process.

To mix the ingredients, first fill the bottle containing the sensitizer with distilled water and shake it well, until the sensitizer is completely dissolved. Pour the sensitizer into the Encosol-1 emulsion, and stir with a wooden or plastic spoon until the fluids are thoroughly blended. Add the dye solution, if desired, and mix thoroughly. Once mixed, the emulsion will last about 3 months at room temperature, and about 6 months if kept under refrigeration.

Raysol Universal Sensitizer, made by the Advance Process Company, is a diazo-base sensitizer that can substitute for ammonium bichromate with regular screen emulsions. When used according to directions, it exhibits the same characteristics as other diazo-sensitized emulsions.

Bichromate-Sensitized Photo Emulsion   Bichromate-sensitized photo emulsions consist of an emulsion base (a heavy, blue, gluelike solution) and the sensitizing solution of ammonium bichromate and water. Ammonium bichromate (dichromate) is sold as dry, orange crystals that must be dissolved in water before being blended with the emulsion base. To make the solution, mix 4 ounces of crystals with 1 quart of lukewarm water. When stored in an amber or light-proof container, this solution will keep for many months without refrigeration until it is mixed with the base.

The solution of dissolved crystals and the emulsion base should be mixed together in a 1 to 5 ratio. The resulting bright green solution should be used within 6 hours. It is therefore a good idea to mix only enough to coat the screen or screens you plan to work on right away. Discard any leftover solution, and mix a fresh supply when it is needed.

Applying Direct
Photo Emulsion to the Screen

Since photo emulsions make the screen sensitive to light, they should be applied to the screen in a dimly lit space and dried in complete darkness or in a darkroom with a yellow or red safelight.

The most efficient way to apply the emulsion to the screen is to use a scoop coater. The coater has a trough that holds a quantity of emulsion and deposits a thin, even layer of it on the fabric. If you are working with a variety of screen sizes, you will need several scoop coaters of different sizes. The scoop coaters should fit conveniently within the frame and be able to coat each side of the screen in one pass.

Place the cleaned screen against a wall or table at a slight angle. Fill the scoop coater to about three-quarters of its capacity, and, starting at the lower edge, tilt the coating edge toward the fabric so that the emulsion begins to pour onto the screen (Fig. 72). Move the

72. Coating the screen with direct emulsion, using a scoop coater under subdued light.

coater up toward the top edge of the screen. When you reach the top, tilt the coater downward, so that the extra emulsion flows back into it. Repeat the operation, then turn the screen over and coat the other side. Allow the screen to dry in a dark place, then apply two additional coats to the bottom, letting each coat dry in between, and one more to the top. If possible, apply each coat at right angles to the previous coat.

Five or more thin coats of the emulsion are preferable to fewer heavy coats because better stencils are produced. If the final coating is too thin, the exposure will be influenced by the fabric mesh, resulting in saw-toothed edges. Since the exposure is made through the bottom of the screen (that is, the side that will come in contact with the printing paper), two extra coats of emulsion on that side ensure that the stencil will be unaffected by the screen mesh.

The thickness in the ink deposit also can be controlled by the thickness of the coating on the bottom of the screen. The thicker the coating, the heavier will be the ink layer that is printed. It must also be remembered that the thicker the coating, the longer the exposure time needed to burn in the image.

The Photographic Positive

Exposure for all types of photo emulsions—both direct and indirect—is always made with a positive image. A copy camera, although certainly a great asset to any workshop, is not a prerequisite to producing creative work with photographic images. Much can be accomplished with a photographic enlarger, a good lens, and a little ingenuity on the part of the screenprinter.

The object of darkroom work is to obtain a photographic positive the same size as the final image on the screen. For example, when a 35mm negative is placed in an enlarger and an exposure is made on another sheet of film (such as Kodalith Orthochromatic film), the result is an extremely high-contrast black-and-white positive enlargement without gray values. This is called a *line shot*. Type, lettering, and all black-and-white line illustrations are line shots (discussed earlier in this chapter).

When a tonal image is to be reproduced photographically, it must be made into a halftone positive. In this case, the light passing through the negative in the enlarger must then shine through a halftone screen that has been placed in contact with the Kodalith film. The tonal values of the 35mm negative are broken up by the lines of the screen into a series of black and white dots of varying sizes. These optically simulate the tonal values of the original negative. The fineness or coarseness of the screen is determined by the number of lines per inch. Until fairly recently, a 65-line screen was used for most screen process halftone work. Today, however, with new screens and emulsions available, halftones of 133 lines and more per inch have been printed successfully. The recent development of the *mezzotint screen* has opened up great possibilities for color separation work, without the disadvantage of the *moiré* pattern that can appear when two or more screens are combined (Fig. 87).

The Handmade Positive

A hand-drawn positive on a transparent or translucent material allows you to achieve excellent results with direct or indirect photo emulsions, even if you do not have access to a copy camera or other expensive darkroom equipment.

The drawing should be made with an opaque substance. Kodak Photo Opaquing solution is ideal and can be applied with a brush or thinned with water for use in a ruling pen. Other substances— such as black poster ink, India ink, ordinary graphite pencil, litho pencils, and crayon—also serve for a variety of textural effects. Prestype letters on an acetate backing form an excellent positive for poster work and lettering of all sizes and styles.

Several kinds of materials make good drawing supports for handmade positives. Three of the best are transparent frosted acetate, translucent vellum, and frosted Mylar. Although more expensive, frosted Mylar is ideal for hand-drawn images. It is dimensionally stable, does not wrinkle, and transmits light exceptionally well. India ink will not "crawl" on its surface. With register guides, a series of Mylar sheets can be superimposed for multicolor work. A light table is necessary for accurate alignment.

Contact Paper Transfer

Magazine transfers on clear contact paper can be used to make photo positives or finished images to be applied to other surfaces. The image is set face down on clear contact paper and rubbed with a burnisher. The contact paper and image are then placed in lukewarm water until the paper is soft enough to be removed easily by gentle rubbing. The ink from the image remains on the contact paper, which then can be used as a photo positive capable of reproducing the original with surprising fidelity. Laminating film made by the Douglas Stewart Company is a very good material for this purpose.

Xerox Transfer

Black-and-white Xerox copy images can be transferred to other surfaces, including paper, fabric, and glass. Though a Xerox machine uses an electrostatic transfer system that works on any type of paper, paper made by Nekoosa seems to work best for transferring purposes. The Xerox copy image is placed face down on the receiving surface, and the back is rubbed with a wad of cotton dampened with acetone. Once the image has been dampened evenly, the back of it is scraped with a wood or metal straightedge (acetone has a solvent effect on plastic). This operation offsets the Xerox image that has partially dissolved onto the other surface. Because the paper will stretch, the back should be scraped only once to avoid double images. If used on translucent vellum the process will produce excellent photo positives.

Exposure

Exposure takes place with the sensitized screen and the photographic positive in the closest possible contact. Exposure time is governed by several factors: the sensitivity of the emulsion, the thickness of the coating on the screen, the strength of the light source, and its distance from the screen. The ultraviolet end of the light spectrum has the greatest effect on photo emulsions, and any light source that is high in ultraviolet light will work. Carbon arc lamps, pulsed zenon, cool fluorescent lights, and black lights all have high outputs of ultraviolet light (Fig. 73).

In recent years new kinds of lamps have come onto the market which are high in ultraviolet output and therefore useful for screen exposures. These include mercury vapor sun lamps, quartz iodine lights, and special "ghost arc" mercury vapor lamps which can be purchased in units of 1000, 2000, and 5000 watt output. These latter lamps, although expensive, considerably shorten exposure times because of their intensity. They also produce a point-light source for accurate rendering of fine details, without the harmful ozone and carbon monoxide produced by carbon arc lamps.

If a single point-light source is used, such as a single carbon arc lamp, it is important that all parts of the image be illuminated equally. The optimum distance from light source to emulsion is the same as the diagonal of the image. This diagonal can be determined simply by measuring. For example, if an image measures 18 by 24 inches, the diagonal is 30 inches. The light source, therefore, should be 30 inches from the positive and the emulsion-covered screen for maximum yet even illumination (Fig. 74). If the light source is closer, the exposure will be uneven and a "hot spot" will result; if farther away, illumination will be distributed evenly, but—since less light will reach the screen—exposure time must be longer.

A screen given six coats of emulsion needs twice the exposure time of a screen coated only three times. The exposure must be sufficient to harden the emulsion to the fabric, for otherwise the entire emulsion—including the nonimage areas—will dissolve from the screen during the washout procedure.

If a single 30-amp carbon lamp is placed at a distance of 30 inches from a screen with five coats of emulsion, the ideal exposure time would be about 5 to 8 minutes.

An exposure unit (Fig. 75) made from a series of black-light or cool-white fluorescent lights, in rows 3 to 4 inches apart and about 4

73. A photographic image
by Romare Bearden
is exposed in a vacuum frame
to a carbon arc lamp.

inches below a plate glass support, will provide a good exposure source. An even simpler arrangement can be made using a flat surface, such as a table top, that is smaller than the frame. Set the frame, bottom side up, on the table, so that the screen rests directly on the surface and the frame extends beyond the table's edge. Place the positive transparency on top of the sensitized screen, and cover it with a sheet of glass. The glass provides enough weight to ensure good contact between the screen and the positive. Use two photofloods at 45-degree angles to each other and at least 3 feet from the glass to provide good illumination. Since these lamps will produce heat, direct a fan at the glass to keep it cool and prevent it from cracking. A fairly long exposure time will be necessary, because the photofloods give considerably less ultraviolet output than either the fluorescents or the arc lamps. With the two 250-watt bulbs placed about 4 feet from the screen, exposure time should be in the range of 10 to 15 minutes.

The best type of exposure unit is one with a vacuum frame to ensure close contact between the positive and the emulsion-coated screen. Two basic kinds are available. The Polycot vacuum unit holds the entire screen and frame and tilts up for exposure to a

below left: 74. The optimum distance
between the exposure unit
and a single light source
is the same as the diagonal measurement
of the image area (the length of c).

below right: 75. An exposure unit
can be made easily.

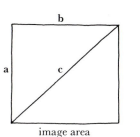

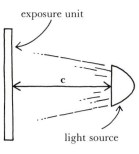

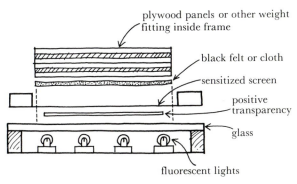

plywood panels or other weight
fitting inside frame

black felt or cloth

sensitized screen

positive
transparency

glass

fluorescent lights

separate light source. The Polylite vacuum unit has fluorescents in a light table arrangement on which the positive and screen are placed and covered with a rubber-backed frame.

Washout

Exposure to ultraviolet light hardens the emulsion and renders it insoluble in water. The unexposed parts of the image, which represent the positive printing areas, are then washed from the screen with a spray of warm water, about 110°F (Fig. 76). Special spray pumps fitted with high-pressure nozzles remove soft, unexposed emulsion quickly from the screen. An ordinary garden hose with an adjustable spray nozzle can be used safely for most work, but to remove the emulsion from fine airbrush-like images, a high-pressure unit is necessary. If the unexposed emulsion is not removed completely by the spray, the image will have ragged edges. After the washout, a cold-water spray will harden the remaining emulsion.

After inspecting the screen closely to ensure that the washout was thorough and complete, blot it with clean newsprint or blotting paper, then place it directly in front of a fan and dry it quickly with a stream of cool air. Check the dry screen by holding it against a light source. Touch up any pinholes with water-soluble blockout, glue, or Kodak Red Photo Opaque.

Indirect Film Technique

Presensitized films such as Ulano HiFi Green, HiFi Blue, Colonial Fine Star, McGraw Colorgraph No. 4570, and Autotype Super Star No. 1 are all excellent for indirect photo screen use. They are composed of a thin, sensitized gelatin layer, adhered to a clear polyester or vinyl backing sheet. Exposure is made directly and through the backing sheet, using a photographic positive or hand-drawn positive image. Exposure, development, and washout are all done in the darkroom, and the film is then adhered to the screen. It is especially important that the screen fabric (preferably silk or multifilament polyester) be clean and properly roughened for good adhesion. Monofilament fabrics, if used, should be scoured thor-

76. Washing the unexposed areas from the screen shown in Figure 73.

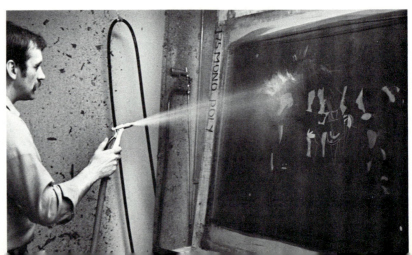

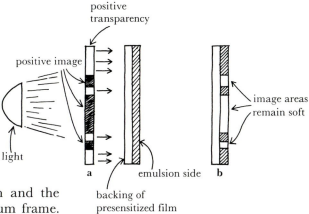

77. Light travels through the positive transparency, then through the backing sheet to the emulsion side of the film (a). After exposure, the image areas remain soft to permit washout (b).

positive transparency

positive image

light

image areas remain soft

a   emulsion side   b

backing of presensitized film

oughly with abrasive and detergent. The indirect film and the transparent positive can be placed in an ordinary vacuum frame.

Presensitized films should be opened only under very subdued light, such as red or yellow safelights, and never should be left open in daylight or under fluorescents. Cut a piece of film an inch or so larger than the positive image, and replace the rest in the container.

Exposure

Exposure is not emulsion-to-emulsion, as it is with most other contact procedures, but must be made through the transparent backing. Light must travel first through the transparent or hand-drawn positive, and then through the transparent backing sheet to reach the gelatin emulsion (Fig. 77). The light coming through the backing sheet hardens the gelatin as it makes contact with the backing, causing the gelatin to adhere to the backing temporarily. Exposure from the emulsion side will leave the emulsion soft where it contacts the backing, and it will separate from the backing during development. If you are unsure which side is the emulsion side, scrape a corner of each side with a knife. On the emulsion side, some of the gelatin will be scraped off.

The basic exposure time for presensitized film is approximately 3 minutes when using a single 30-amp carbon arc lamp at a distance of 30 inches. Exposure time is always governed by the strength of the light source and its distance from the film. If you are unsure of exposure times, make a step-wedge series of exposures on a test image to find the best image resolution. Good contact between positive and film is essential. A vacuum unit is an ideal aid (Fig. 78).

78. Using a Polylite vacuum exposure unit.

Development

A special two-part developer for the Ulano HiFi Green and HiFi Blue is available in premeasured envelopes. Dissolve the contents of each envelope in 16 ounces of water at 68 to 70°F. Then pour the mixture into a tray large enough to accommodate an entire sheet of exposed film. Immerse the film in the developer with the emulsion side up for $1\frac{1}{2}$ to $2\frac{1}{2}$ minutes (Fig. 79). At this point, carefully remove the film from the tray, since the emulsion is soft and can be scratched easily with a fingernail. Place the film emulsion side up on a flat sheet of glass or other surface inclined into a sink. Spray the surface with a gentle current of warm water, 110 to 115°F, until the image areas appear clearly defined and all the softened emulsion has been washed away. Spray briefly with cold water to firm up the film. It is now ready for adhesion to the screen.

The developer for the Autotype Super Star No. 1 consists of a 3-percent hydrogen peroxide solution. After exposure the film is developed in a tray for approximately 1 minute, sprayed with warm water, and adhered to the screen in the same manner as the Ulano films.

The McGraw Colorgraph Film No. 4570 does not need a developer solution. Instead, it may be sprayed with warm water directly after exposure. This film has an expiration date stamped on the wrapper. If used after that date, it should be developed with a hydrogen peroxide solution, in the same manner as the Autotype Superstar No. 1.

Adhering the Film to the Screen

Immediately after spraying with cold water, place the film emulsion side up on a smooth, level surface. Lower the screen gently onto the film. Blot the screen immediately with clean newsprint, maintaining a light, even pressure (Fig. 80). This will blot excess moisture from the surface and push the softened emulsion into the screen. Change the newsprint several times, using each sheet only once on each side, so that any emulsion that might come off onto the newsprint will not be deposited back on the screen. Areas that have adhered well will immediately appear darker.

below left: 79. The film is developed emulsion side up.

below right: 80. The presensitized film is gently adhered to the screen after development and washout.

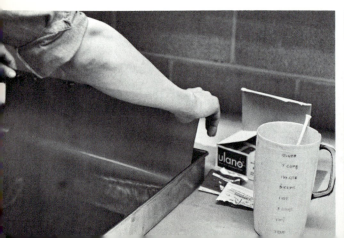

Place the screen in an upright position, and dry it with a fan. When it is dry, peel the backing slowly from the screen; the gelatin film will remain adhered to the screen. Hold the screen up to the light, and check for any imperfections. Touch up, if necessary, with water-soluble blockout. The screen is now ready for the next stage—the printing process.

Carbon Tissue Technique

Carbon tissue is a gelatin and pigment film adhered to a paper backing sheet. It was first used in the late 1800s for photogravure intaglio printing and, by the 1920s, for photographic screenprinting.

This film, which comes unsensitized, is one of the least expensive of all the photo films and has the advantage of lasting indefinitely without spoilage or loss of quality. When exposed and manipulated correctly, it reproduces extremely fine, sharp, and crisp detail as well as any of the presensitized or direct photo emulsions.

Following are the steps in its use:

1. First, unroll the carbon tissue and cut a piece to fit the screen at least an inch larger than the photo positive image to be used.
2. Place the tissue in a tray into which has been poured a 2- or 3-percent solution of either ammonium bichromate or potassium bichromate. This is the sensitizing solution for the tissue and is mixed by adding 2 or 3 grams of dry crystalline bichromate to 1000 grams (1 liter) of water.
3. Completely immerse the tissue emulsion side up until it begins to uncurl and lie perfectly flat in the tray. The temperature of the solution should not rise above 70°F or the tissue will begin to dissolve. (Try to maintain the temperature in the 50–60°F range if possible.) Allow the tissue to absorb the bichromate sensitizer for 2 to 3 minutes.
4. Next, carefully remove the tissue from the solution and place face down onto a sheet of clear, 5 or 7 mil polyester or Mylar plastic. Roll out lightly on a flat surface to remove any air bubbles, and blot the back to remove any excess sensitizer.
5. While the carbon image is still wet, place the positive image on the clear polyester or Mylar side of the tissue, and then put the entire "sandwich" in a vacuum frame for exposure. Because the tissue is being exposed while in a wet state, exposure will take longer than in other processes. Any of the previously mentioned light sources can be used. Exposure takes place first through the positive, then through the clear plastic onto the gelatin film.
6. After exposure, immerse the tissue and plastic in a tray of very warm water (approximately 110°F). In a few minutes the emulsion will begin to ooze from between the plastic and paper. The paper backing can then be peeled away, and the tissue rocked in the warm water solution or sprayed with warm water.

7. When all the details of the image appear sharply defined, change the spray of warm water to cold. This helps to firm up the emulsion.
8. Put the tissue emulsion side up on a flat surface and gently lower a clean, carefully prepared screen onto the emulsion. The image can be seen from the top of the screen as it becomes imbedded into the mesh. Gently blot the screen with clean newsprint, then allow the carbon tissue to dry thoroughly. Drying may be speeded up with a fan.
9. When it is dry, remove the clear plastic film from the adhered stencil by starting first from a corner. The remainder of the screen is blocked out and then checked. At that point, it is ready for printing.

Removal of the carbon tissue after printing can be done by spraying with very hot water and then scrubbing with a stiff brush after all traces of ink have been removed. If the film is stubborn, an enzyme cleaner may be used.

Other Photographic Techniques

Duotone Printing

An overall color cast, as well as added richness and depth, can be given to a normal black-and-white image by means of the *duotone* process. This involves printing the image first in one color, then in black or a second color. The first halftone positive is placed on the screen and rotated against the light until the *moiré* pattern disappears (usually when the halftone is at an angle of about $22\frac{1}{2}$ degrees to the threads of the fabric). (See p. 96.) The second halftone positive should be made so that its halftone pattern is about 20 to 30 degrees from that of the first. Your eye is the best guide.

Continuous-Tone Screenprinting

The recently developed *continuous-tone* screenprinting technique considerably expands the possibilities of the screenprinted image. A continuous-tone negative (one that has not been screened) is placed in the enlarger and exposed through a *mezzotint* screen onto sheets of ortho film, using a step exposure system not unlike the posterization technique.

The Mezzotint Screen Although recently introduced, the mezzotint screen is becoming increasingly popular for screenprinting. It can be used for making black-and-white halftones, as well as for color separations. Its great advantage over the halftone screen is that it has a random dot pattern, instead of a regular dot pattern, eliminating the need to angle screens in color process work (Fig. 81).

81. James Rosenquist. *Starfish,* detail. 1974.
Screenprint poster with mezzotint screen.
Courtesy Graphicstudio,
University of South Florida, Tampa.

The finest mezzotint screen suitable for screenprinting is a 150-line
(equivalent rating) grid.

Continuous-Tone Technique   All image planning should take
place at the camera stage, when the greatest control is possible.
Therefore, the number of step exposures to be made should be
decided in advance. With a 150-line mezzotint screen, a very
smooth tonal gradation can be achieved in three steps. Printing
conditions must be optimum to reproduce fine detail faithfully. If
five steps and a 75-line screen are used, it is possible to produce the
continuous tone effect with even softer transitions.

The ink employed for the continuous tone is important. Each
step of printing must use a transparent film of ink that prints cleanly
and thinly. (The thin-film ethyl cellulose inks are excellent.) Even
more important is the choice of transparent base, which must be
absolutely clear and colorless. Most extender bases have too much
opacity to be successful. A very small percentage of ink is added to
the transparent base, because the tone produced will depend on the
number of steps in the series. In three-step printing, the overprinting
of the three tones should produce accurately the darkest tone
desired. With more steps, the transition between the deep tones and
highlights will be smoother. From the point of view of production, it
would be convenient to use the same ink tone for each printing step;
however, the ink may be intensified or lightened at any stage to
control the tonal range.

82. Three Kodalith positives, top to bottom: one underexposed, one normally exposed, and one overexposed.

83. The three positives shown in Figure 82 were placed on the screens with presensitized film.

84. This completed posterized image was made by printing the screens in Figure 83. Exact registration is critical to the success of such a print.

Posterization

Posterization is a photographic technique utilizing variable exposures and a continuous-tone negative to reproduce the positive images in a series of steps. The step positives are then exposed onto different screens and printed in a selected range of colors or tones, producing highly dramatic images with sharp, delineated areas of color. Posterization techniques require some darkroom experience, since the work depends on photographic manipulation of the image.

The first requirement in a multistep posterization is a good-quality continuous-tone negative with an extensive range of middle tones. The negative can be 35mm, 2¼ by 2¼ inches, or 4 by 5 inches. It is placed in an enlarger, which is then focused to the exact size desired. The image is exposed onto orthochromatic film such as Kodalith, Dupont Ortho-Litho, or Ansco litho film. This reduces the gradated tones of the negative into a high-contrast, black-and-white positive. In a simplified three-step procedure, for example, three exposures can be made—one underexposed, one with normal exposure, and one overexposed. The three resulting positives will be considerably different from one another in tone and contour (Fig. 82). They are used to produce images on three different screens, with either the direct or the indirect photo technique (Fig. 83). The screens are then printed with a selection of colors in careful register (Fig. 84). In addition to using variable exposures, the development time can be increased or decreased to add further variance to the images. Orthochromatic films have considerable latitude in both exposure and development times.

A greater range and subtlety can be produced in the image by increasing the number of steps in the procedure, and by working with a positive and negative image to produce the step exposures.

SIX

Printing on Paper and Hard Surfaces

Screenprinting Inks

A wide variety of inks have been formulated in recent years to meet the needs of the growing field of screenprinting. In addition to the usual oil- or cellulose-base inks for printing on paper and similar materials, inks have been designed for printing on glass, plastics, metal, and textiles (Fig. 85). The printing surface need not be flat—it is possible to screen an image onto glassware, plastic containers, and ceramic ware (directly or with the aid of decal paper). In the electronics industry, printed circuits often are screened onto copper-clad phenolic with acid-resistant ink, and then etched in acid. Epoxy resins, which form some of the strongest and most durable bonds between two surfaces, have been formulated into inks that can be printed on almost any surface, including metal, glass, and wood, and are completely weather resistant. Vinyl inks also have been used more and more to screen patterns and designs on vinyl products. The ink dissolves the supporting vinyl material slightly, and as it dries it becomes an integral part of the item itself.

Paper, however, remains the supporting material for most of the creative screenprinting done today. Poster inks (both mat and glossy) are used more often than any other type of ink for artistic work of all kinds, although other types of inks (enamels, lacquers, and fluorescent inks) are sometimes introduced for special effects.

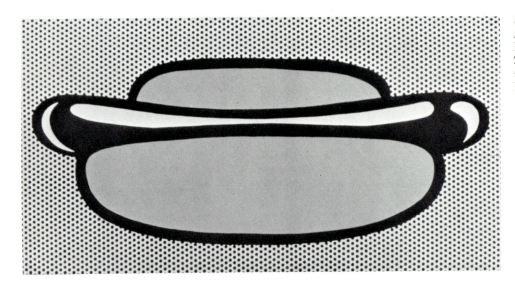

85. Roy Lichtenstein.
Hot Dog. 1964.
Baked enamel on steel,
2 × 4″ (5 × 10 cm).
Courtesy Leo Castelli Gallery,
New York.

Characteristics of Screenprinting Inks

An ink must have certain characteristics in order to be suitable for screenprinting. It must be nonoily, short and buttery in consistency, and have sufficient body for sharp, even printing. Shortness is the quality that prevents drag on the squeegee and makes the ink break from the screen without leaving "strings." An oily ink will leave oil rings or *halos* around images.

If you modify an ink for any reason, keep these basic characteristics in mind so that the proper printing qualities will be maintained. If, for example, a small amount of lithographic ink is added to some screen ink or to a transparent base, there will be little change in the printing characteristics. As more is added, however, the tackiness of the litho ink will make it more difficult to print and will produce considerable drag on the squeegee. If a dry powder—such as aluminum stearate, magnesium carbonate, or cornstarch—is added to the ink, the body of the ink will be increased. If the quantity is too great, the thickness of the ink will be unsuitable for proper printing, the final image brittle, and the colors dull. In most cases, it is best to stay within the manufacturer's specific recommendations when making modifications to the ink.

All screen inks consist of a vehicle (also called the binder) and pigment (or other coloring matter). The vehicle generally determines the drying time of the ink. Cellulose poster inks and lacquers dry very quickly—usually in 15 to 30 minutes. Enamels may take from 4 to 12 hours or more, depending on the specific ink and the humidity of the air.

The drying itself takes place in a different way for each particular ink. Ink dries by evaporation, oxidation, polymerization, penetration, or by a combination of these.

The inks that dry by evaporation include poster inks, lacquers, vinyls, and water-base inks. As the solvents evaporate, the pigment and a resinous binder are left on the printed surface.

Enamels and other oil-base inks dry primarily by means of oxidation, with some evaporation and polymerization taking place. Oxidation is a process in which oxygen from the atmosphere unites with the ingredients of the ink, slowly transforming the liquid ink into a solid. Drying agents, made from the metallic salts of cobalt, lead, manganese, or zinc, speed up the drying of enamel inks.

Polymerization occurs when certain substances unite to form a molecular crosslinking system. This takes place simultaneously throughout all the molecules of ink. Epoxy inks, which dry in this way, usually contain epoxy resin with pigment and a catalyst. When these are mixed together, polymerization begins. These inks dry much faster than enamels, and heat speeds the drying even more. (One type of epoxy ink dries only when heated.)

Some inks are formulated to dry primarily by penetration. This method of drying relies on a highly absorbent paper or fabric to retain the bulk of the vehicle and pigment. Some water-containing textile inks appear dry to the touch immediately after printing because the ink is absorbed into the fabric so quickly. The water actually evaporates at a rate that depends on the humidity of the surrounding area.

Types of Screenprinting Inks

Poster Inks   Poster inks usually are formulated from a base of nitrocellulose or ethyl cellulose. Under normal conditions they dry in 15 to 20 minutes, primarily by means of solvent evaporation. Printing always should take place in a well-ventilated area. Poster inks are available in mat and gloss finishes and are used widely for printing on paper or cardboard. They are heavy, intense, and for the most part opaque, although it is now easy to control the ink's thickness and light-reflecting qualities. If mixed with transparent base the colors will become increasingly lighter and more transparent. When more than 50 percent base is mixed with the ink, it is a good idea to add a small amount of binding varnish to improve adhesion and increase the flexibility of the printed surface.

Mat poster inks on large flat areas of color are particularly susceptible to scuff marks. A small amount of glossy ink or varnish will help to alleviate this problem. Mat and glossy inks also can be mixed together to achieve a semigloss finish.

Paper has a considerable influence on the finish and durability of the ink. Glossy ink printed on a highly absorbent surface will dry to a dull finish; on a nonabsorbent stock it will dry to a high sheen. This can present problems in color printing, because the first color may dry to a dull finish, and any overprinted colors may dry to a higher gloss. To overcome this difficulty, a sealer coat composed of

60 percent transparent base, 30 percent opaque white, and 10 percent binding varnish can be printed first over the entire image area. Another solution to this problem is to cover the entire image with clear varnish after printing.

Enamel Inks   Enamel inks are characterized by their toughness, their ability to adhere to a variety of surfaces (including glass and metal), and their brilliance and flexibility. They dry very slowly, however, often taking up to 12 hours or more depending on temperature and humidity conditions. Although mat-finish enamels are available, enamel inks usually are associated with high-gloss surfaces. They are bright and luminous when mixed with an enamel transparent base. A heavy buildup of ink is also possible in color printing, creating a surface tactility.

Fluorescent Inks   Fluorescent inks reflect light. They also convert wavelengths of light to the wavelength of their particular color, thus producing their characteristic glow. Unlike phosphorescent paint, which glows in complete darkness, fluorescents are activated by a black (ultraviolet) light or other light source. Since they are semitransparent, they achieve maximum effectiveness only when printed on white stock.

In the case of a print to be made on black or other dark paper, screen white opaque ink on the image areas first. Fluorescent inks have limited permanence but can be made to last longer if protected from sunlight.

Lacquer Inks   Lacquer inks dry very quickly and work with all types of photo stencils, water-base blockout, and glue solutions. They should not be used with lacquer stencils, lacquer blockout, or shellac, however. (Lacquer slowly dissolves shellac.) Good ventilation is important when using lacquer inks because of their odor and the volatility of their solvents. Lacquers are characterized by their high gloss, acid resistance, and rugged durability.

Vinyl Inks   Developed expressly for printing on vinyl, vinyl inks come in both mat and glossy finishes and can be mixed for any degree of finish in between. A special vinyl base is available to reduce the ink to any degree of transparency.

Vinyl inks dry by evaporation in about 15 minutes after printing (or slightly longer in humid conditions). It is imperative to have good ventilation, not only to speed drying, but also to disperse toxic fumes from the evaporating solvents. Use lacquer thinner as the solvent for cleaning up after printing. Strict fire precautions should be observed, since the inks and their solvents are highly flammable. One excellent characteristic of these inks is that they do not dry in the screen. Vinyl inks can be left for long periods of time without clogging the screen.

Inks Made with Oil Colors   Oil colors can be mixed with transparent base to produce brilliantly colored improvised inks. The more oil color used, the longer the drying time of the ink.

Inks Suitable for Vacuum-Formed Images   Inks that retain flexibility, have good adhesion characteristics, and can be effectively printed over each other are used for vacuum-formed printing. They are available from major manufacturers. The dye or pigmented base should be selected so that it has a chemical similarity or affinity for the surface on which it will be used. There are inks for styrene, epoxies, vinyls, acrylics, and phenolics, among others. Acrylic inks, however, are compatible with most plastics for vacuum-formed printed works.

Ink Modifiers

There are a number of additives that modify the qualities of ink. Most modern inks have been formulated to be used directly from the can. A modifier is sometimes necessary, though, to obtain certain printing qualities.

Transparent Base   The most common modifying agent is transparent base, which acts as an extender for ink and, in any quantity, as an agent for making ink transparent. It is heavy-bodied and adds *shortness* to the ink. The natural lubricating character of transparent base often improves the printing qualities of the ink. Each type of ink—lacquer, vinyl, enamel, or poster ink—has its own particular transparent base.

Extender Base   A neutral bulking medium, extender base increases the working quantity of a given amount of ink without changing its color. This base imparts a certain opacity to an ink, which means that it is unsuitable for use as a transparent medium where absolute clarity of the transparencies is desired. If extender is added to ink in more than a 1 to 3 ratio, the ink has a tendency to become brittle and chalky. A small amount of binding varnish will improve the ink's flexibility and adhesion.

Binding Varnish   An additive especially effective with poster inks is clear binding varnish, which increases the flexibility of an ink. Binding varnish improves the ink's adhesion to the printing surface and helps prevent chalking of the ink, especially on very absorbent surfaces. If transparent base or extender base comprises 50 percent or more of an ink, it is a good idea to add approximately 5 to 10 percent of binding varnish.

Toners   Toners are highly concentrated colors useful for intensifying or tinting an image. A small quantity of toner added to a transparent base produces rich yet transparent colors. Toners cannot be used alone but are formulated strictly as additives to other colors or bases.

Gloss Varnish   Gloss varnish functions either as an additive or as an overall varnish to increase the glossiness of flat ink. When printed over the image, it gives an even gloss and intensifies flat colors.

Flattening Powders   A number of powders help to flatten an ink and increase its body. Cornstarch, magnesium carbonate, aluminum hydrate, and aluminum stearate all can be added to inks in small quantities for this purpose. However, if too much powder is included, the surface may become chalky and the screen clogged.

Reducers   The most common form of reducer for any particular ink is its solvent. A small amount of mineral spirits or paint thinner, for example, will dilute poster inks, making them more fluid and increasing their tendency to be absorbed into the surface of the paper stock. Some reducers, such as kerosene, also will slow the drying of the ink and lessen its tendency to clog the screen. Each manufacturer makes a reducer for each of its inks.

Retarders   Retarders slow the drying of the ink, reducing the viscosity and promoting greater ink flow at the same time. They help prevent clogging of the screen and, in addition, are invaluable for hand printing.

The Color Palette

Every manufacturer offers a wide range of colors for each type of screenprinting ink. For a small screenprinting workshop, it is wise to limit the purchase of inks to the type or types most frequently needed. For example, if the bulk of the work is fine art printing on paper, 90 percent of the printing probably will be done with flat poster inks. In a student workshop, where many people print, limiting the types of ink available may help to eliminate the danger of someone accidentally mixing incompatible inks. In any event, keep the printing area well organized and all equipment properly stored and labeled (Fig. 86).

Since poster inks are used more than any other type of ink for printing on paper or board, it is a good idea to acquaint yourself with the color charts put out by each manufacturer. Flat and glossy poster inks can be mixed in equal parts to produce semigloss colors. When mixing inks, it is best to stay with one brand. Gallon containers of flat poster inks and quarts of glossy inks in the same color range are the most convenient initial investment. It is also advisable to have several gallon containers of transparent base to extend individual colors and make them transparent.

86. Squeegee storage area showing an efficient use of space.

Plate 7. Frank Stella. *York Factory II.* 1973.
Fifty-three-color screenprint, $18^{7}/_{16} \times 44^{7}/_{16}''$ (46 × 111 cm).
Courtesy Gemini G.E.L., Los Angeles.

Plate 8. Alan Shields.
Sun, Moon, Title Page. 1971.
Dye, silkscreen on paper
and thread; 26″ (65 cm) square.
Courtesy Paula Cooper Gallery, New York.

Plate 9. Robert Rauschenberg.
Third panel from *Star Quarters*. 1971.
Silkscreened mirrored Plexiglas, 4′ (1.22 m) square.
Courtesy Multiples, Inc., New York.

All colors theoretically can be produced with the three primary colors—red, yellow, and blue. In practice, however, this is only partially true. The choice of primaries determines the brilliance of the secondary colors. To obtain a brilliant green, for example, the yellow must be cool and not tend to orange, and the blue also should be cool and not tend to purple. Peacock blue and primrose yellow make a crisp, brilliant green. Ultramarine blue, which has a purple tinge, will yield a dull green, and if it is mixed with a warm, slightly orange shade of yellow, will give a considerably more muddy green. On the other hand, ultramarine blue mixed with cerise will result in a clean, brilliant purple. Peacock blue mixed with fire red, however, will produce a muddy purplish color.

Because of these characteristics, it is necessary to have a range of colors in addition to the primaries. This range should include a warm and cool variant of each of the primaries, black, opaque white, a good transparent white, and an extender. A basic inventory of color might be:

o lemon yellow (warm)
o primrose yellow (cool)
o yellow ochre (warm earth color)
o fire red (warm red-orange)
o cerise (cool alizarin red)
o peacock blue (cool blue, slightly greenish)
o ultramarine blue (warm blue, slightly purple)
o opaque white
o black
o transparent base (modifier)
o binding varnish (modifier)

Color Mixing and Matching

Before beginning the actual printing, premix the exact color you desire in sufficient quantity for the whole job. Nothing is more annoying than having to interrupt the printing because enough ink was not mixed initially. This would not be a problem if all colors were used directly from the container, of course. But with most color screenprinting, each individual color is unique (Pl. 7, p. 93). Each one must be mixed separately and matched to a color sample.

Color matching involves good visual perception. The screenprint relies ultimately on the *appearance* of the mixed color, rather than on any scientific device for determining a correct match. A 3-by-4-inch piece of black paper or showcard board with two small openings about an inch apart serves as an excellent aid in matching two colors. Place each color under one of the openings. The card isolates them from surrounding colors and allows you to make a close comparison of the match. When using opaque colors, a dab of the mixed color on a piece of printing paper gives a fair indication of

87. A moiré pattern results from the misalignment of two screens.

the color as it will print. However, wait for the ink to dry before judging the match.

This method is inaccurate for transparent colors, however, because the final color will be influenced by the thickness of the ink layer. It is important to proof transparent colors under the same conditions that will be encountered in the final printing. This means using the same stencil thickness, the same screen fabric, the same paper, and so forth, so that the ink deposit will be identical. The mixing procedure itself is also of great importance when working with transparent colors. The inks must be blended thoroughly, otherwise streaks will show up in the printing. (This defect is less noticeable when using opaque inks.)

A number of clean metal cans, nonporous paper containers, or jars should be kept on hand for mixing and storing inks. Storage containers should have tight covers to prevent the ink from drying. A color sample taped to the outside serves as a useful reference.

Process Colors

Process colors have a finely ground concentration of pigment and are designed to give the cleanest possible transparent colors when overprinted. The colors are process red (magenta), process blue (cyan), and process yellow. For the best results in clarity and sharpness, mix these inks with a heavy-bodied halftone base.

Four-Color Process Work

In normal process work, the areas where each of the three basic colors (red, yellow, and blue) and black appear in the original art work or color transparency must be separated by special filters in a process camera or enlarger. In halftone separations, each color is separated into a series of dots representing its tonal range. The halftone screen must be placed at specific angles for each color in order to prevent the dot patterns of the different colors from printing on top of each other, and to avoid *moiré* patterns.

A *moiré* pattern is an optical effect that results when two regularly patterned surfaces are placed together in such a way that both patterns can be seen simultaneously, yielding a third strong pattern (Fig. 87). The pattern changes with the relationship of one screen or fabric to the other. *Moiré* effects have been used for centuries to produce decorative textiles in which two independent fabrics have been woven together.

However, except when created intentionally, a *moiré* pattern is objectionable to the screenprinter and usually is eliminated in multicolor halftone work. Screenprinters have a special problem, because—in addition to the halftone screens—the fabric itself can produce a *moiré* pattern. As a result, even when a single-color halftone image is to be placed on the screen, it must be angled

88. In this workshop
at Fine Creations, Inc.,
New York,
prints are removed
from the squeegee unit
and placed in a drying rack
a few steps away.

carefully. The halftone positive and the screen are placed together and held up to the light, and the positive is rotated slowly until the pattern disappears. The screen is then marked so that the exposure of the positive takes place in exactly the same position. (When using direct photo emulsion, position marks for the positive should be made before the emulsion is put on the screen.) Some printers avoid *moiré* patterns by stretching the screen in such a way that the strands of fabric are diagonal to the sides of the frame.

In three-color process work, the halftone screens used to make the separation positives are placed at the following angles to the horizontal axis:

yellow	105°
blue	45°
red	75°

In four-color process work, the angles are as follows:

yellow	90°
blue	105°
black	45°
red	75°

Printing Technique

The mechanics of screenprinting are refreshingly simple when compared to other graphic arts processes. The first thing to consider in printing is the convenience of the printing setup. Everything necessary for the printing operation must be easily accessible and arranged to allow the printing to proceed swiftly and without interruption (Fig. 88). Make sure your working space has adequate ventilation to allow the solvents in the ink to evaporate and to speed drying. The supplies you will need include:

o poster, enamel, fluorescent, lacquer, or vinyl ink
o ink modifiers
o cans or jars for storing mixed colors
o soft, clean rags
o paint thinner
o waste printing paper and good printing paper
o squeegees (several sizes to accommodate images)
o drying rack or other drying arrangement
o dowel sticks
o register tabs made of plastic or heavy paper
o a sheet of clear Mylar or acetate
o solvent appropriate to your ink
o sheets of newsprint
o a nylon scrub brush
o acetic acid or vinegar (optional)

Short runs can be handled by a single person who positions the paper, squeegees the ink, and racks each sheet for drying. Long runs are managed best by at least two persons—one who squeegees, and one, or even two, "take-off" assistants to register the paper and rack it after printing. There must be sufficient room for the assistant to register the paper freely and remove each sheet without getting in the way of the printer. The drying racks also should be placed so that each sheet can be racked immediately after it is printed and a steady rhythm maintained.

Select a squeegee larger than the image by at least an inch on either side and smaller than the sides of the frame to glide freely during the printing stroke. Place dowel sticks into holes on either side of the squeegee so that they extend over the frame. These will act as a stop to prevent the squeegee from falling into the ink (Fig. 89). For a one-handed squeegee, nail a short stick to the handle (Fig. 90). Masking tape on the stick can be changed when it becomes covered with ink.

Check to see that all equipment is laid out in a logical manner, and begin by registering a sheet of trial paper. Go through all the motions of printing and racking the paper, to see if any obstruction or impediment exists in the even flow of the work. If so, adjust your setup or procedures to allow the printing process to proceed smoothly and rapidly.

Holding the Paper to the Table

Although a vacuum table is certainly the most efficient instrument for holding the paper firmly during printing, another very useful technique that can be used in the absence of a vacuum table is to

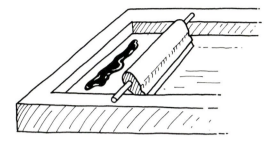

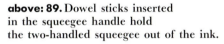

above: 89. Dowel sticks inserted
in the squeegee handle hold
the two-handled squeegee out of the ink.

right: 90. A one-handed squeegee
can be kept out of the ink reservoir
by a stick nailed to the handle.

spray a table top with an adhesive. Blot the adhesive two or three
times with clean sheets of cover stock to reduce the tack. The
adhesive should now have sufficient tack left to hold the paper
down, but not enough to damage it when it is removed after
printing. Fresh adhesive should be sprayed on the table after every
ten or fifteen prints. It is also a good idea to mask any areas of the
table you do not wish to spray.

Estimating the Amount of Ink Needed

Screenprinting ink manufacturers provide an estimate of the coverage of each of their inks, expressed in square feet per gallon for a
particular mesh size. This is a good guide for estimating the amount
of ink needed for a particular job.

The total area to be covered is determined by the size of the
printing area, the number of prints to be made, the size of the screen
mesh, the thickness of the stencil, the condition and hardness of the
squeegee, and the amount of pressure exerted on the squeegee
during printing. A coarse screen mesh allows more ink to flow
through the screen, and a dull or rounded squeegee deposits a
heavier ink layer. Greater pressure on the squeegee results in a
thinner layer of ink.

After estimating the coverage needed for a given run, add a
further 10 to 15 percent to avoid the frustrating and time-consum-
ing task of rematching a color in the middle of a job.

The Flood Stroke

The *flood stroke,* one of the most useful techniques in screenprinting,
is utilized in almost all screenprinting jobs. Immediately before

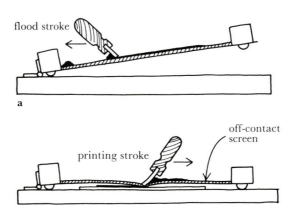

flood stroke

off-contact
screen

printing stroke

a

b

right: 91. Before each print, the screen must be flood coated by pulling the squeegee across the screen to distribute the ink. (a). The printing stroke forces the ink through the screen as the squeegee travels back in the other direction (b).

below: 92. The angle of the squeegee should be 45 degrees. The two squeegees to the left are too vertical or low; the one at right is correct.

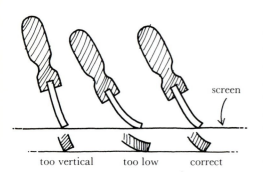

screen

too vertical   too low   correct

each printing stroke, the screen is lifted away from the paper, and ink is distributed over the screen by pulling the squeegee in the opposite direction from the printing stroke. (Before the first flood stroke, pour a quantity of ink across the top or the side of the screen, depending on the direction the squeegee will follow.) Do not apply any pressure in the flood stroke (Fig. 91), since the weight of the squeegee itself is usually sufficient. The flood stroke fills the mesh with ink and prevents the screen from drying. It also prepares the screen for the next stroke. Replenish the ink as necessary while you are printing.

Squeegee Manipulation

Lower the screen into position. Without turning it around, grasp the squeegee firmly with both hands and pull it across the screen. The squeegee should be held at an angle of about 45 degrees from the vertical, in the direction of the stroke (Fig. 92). It makes a slight rasping sound if it is pulled across the screen correctly. Lift the screen immediately, remove the paper, flood coat the screen, and insert another sheet. This sequence should be followed for each print. All screenprinting is actually "off-contact"; that is, the screen rests at least $\frac{1}{8}$ to $\frac{3}{8}$ inch above the paper (depending on the image size) until the moment of printing. Small pieces of cardboard or thumbtacks under the corners of the frame hold the frame off the table. The pressure of the squeegee pulls the screen down to the paper, and after the squeegee has passed, the tension of the screen lifts it up again. If the entire screen rested on the paper during printing, the pull from the squeegee would make it drag across the paper and blur the image slightly.

Except where a heavy buildup of ink is desired, the characteristics of a good screenprint are low buildup of ink, sharp, crisp outlines, and faithful printing of every open detail. This can be achieved only with a sharp squeegee, proper squeegee angle and pressure, taut screens, and good ink. The angle and pressure of the blade are of paramount importance. Whether the squeegee blade is soft, medium, or hard, the optimum angle at which it contacts the screen is 45 degrees. Because the blade bends under pressure, the angle must be watched carefully.

Excessive pressure is unnecessary; it creates too much friction and could lead to a slight distortion of the screen. If the squeegee is too soft, if it is held at the wrong angle or used with too much pressure, the blade may flatten out, causing fuzzy edges and heavy, uneven deposits of ink.

With extremely sharp, hard-edged images, a slight underplay of ink may occur on some edges and cause a slight roughness to appear. After every dozen or so prints, wipe the underside of the screen lightly with a soft, clean cloth.

If printing must be interrupted for any length of time, squeegee the ink left on the screen onto some waste paper to clear the screen; if oil or enamel ink was used, spray both sides with Ink-O-Saver (a light, nondrying oil used to prevent skimming of litho inks). Before resuming printing, wipe both sides of the screen with a clean rag and make several prints on waste paper until the image begins to print perfectly again.

Multiple Passes with the Squeegee

If a faulty impression is made due to running out of ink or some other reason, avoid making a squeegee pass on the same sheet. This always leads to a blurred impression, often necessitating cleaning below the screen as ink offsets underneath. Instead, remove the faulty print, and print it again at the end or when it has dried.

Register Guides

Several types of register guides are available commercially. For the vast majority of prints, however, simple register stops made of heavyweight paper or plastic slightly thicker than the printing stock perform quite well. Cut three tabs approximately $\frac{3}{4}$ by 2 inches, and adhere two to the long side of the baseboard or vacuum table and one to the short side (Fig. 93). Use a little water-soluble glue or

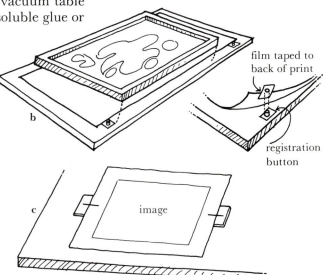

93. Register guides for screenprinting include three-point register tabs (a), register buttons (b), and the T-bar method (c).

film taped to back of print

registration button

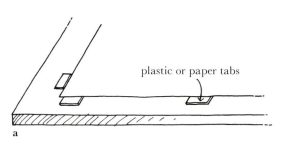

plastic or paper tabs

a

b

c

image

spray adhesive. (Do not use permanent bonding glue.) When in perfect register, the paper will butt up against all three stops. Allow for some extra prints to be made in every edition, because there are always a few prints that will be spoiled due to misregistration or some other cause.

Very large prints can be registered easily by using two metal buttons (commercially available) that are taped to the table top, outside the area covered by the frame. Two small pieces of film or cardboard with a hole punched in each are taped to the back of the printing paper, extending past the edge. (A large margin is needed, for the paper must be trimmed after printing.) The holes in the tabs slip over the buttons on the table top (Fig. 94).

A simple method of registration, also suitable for deckle-edged paper, involves marking the midpoints of the ends of each sheet of paper. Using a sharp pencil, make your marks on the back of the paper. A T and a straight line are drawn on the table top or base, corresponding to opposite ends of the paper. The edge of the paper is lined up against the horizontal of the T, and the midpoint mark on the paper is lined up against the vertical of the T. The midpoint line on the opposite end of the paper is aligned with the straight line registration mark on the table top or base (Fig. 94). Drawbacks to this method (known as the T-bar method) are that the printing paper must always be smaller than the table or baseboard, and a small part of the deckle on some papers will have to be trimmed to ensure accuracy.

Another helpful guide in color work is a clear sheet of Mylar or acetate a few inches larger all around than the printing paper. Once the position for the first color has been established and the register tabs have been set on the baseboard, place the sheet of plastic in position over the image area and the tabs, taping it to prevent it from moving. Print the image onto the plastic sheet, and mark the

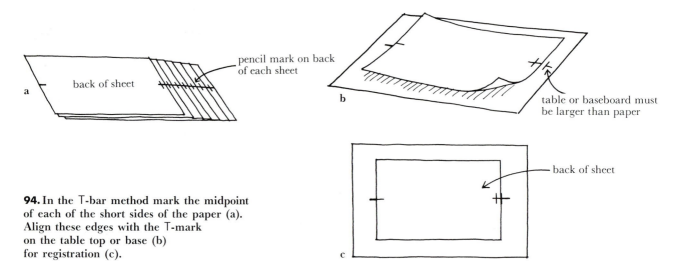

pencil mark on back of each sheet

a   back of sheet

b

table or baseboard must be larger than paper

back of sheet

94. In the T-bar method mark the midpoint of each of the short sides of the paper (a). Align these edges with the T-mark on the table top or base (b) for registration (c).

c

position of the registration guides accurately on it with tape. Remove the plastic, and print with the first color.

When the second screen is ready for printing, tape a sheet of paper to the baseboard and pull a proof. Then position the clear plastic with the first color and registration points accurately on top. New register tabs for the second color, seen through the clear plastic, are then attached to the baseboard. The plastic is removed before printing. This method allows very close registration, and if it is done carefully, little adjustment of the tabs will be necessary.

Registration marks are burned into photographically-made color screens along with the image. Rolls of transparent cellophane register marks can be purchased in negative or positive form from any lithographic supply house and are well worth their small cost. After five or ten trial sheets have been printed with the register marks showing, a tab of masking tape can be placed over these marks on the bottom side of the screen to prevent their appearing in the finished prints of the edition.

Registering on Fully Deckled Paper

Registering against cardboard or plastic tabs is accurate only when the paper has straight edges. The following technique allows close registration on deckled or irregular paper, without requiring registration stops.

Cut a sheet of acetate, or preferably transparent Mylar, several inches larger all around than the printing paper, and hinge one edge to the side or front of the printing baseboard or table with tape. Print the first color onto each sheet of paper and allow the ink to dry. Print the second color onto the Mylar, position the paper under it, then lift the Mylar and print the second color (Fig. 95). Because the Mylar remains hinged to the printing baseboard or

95. A print by Roy Lichtenstein is registered with a Mylar sheet at Styria Studios, New York.

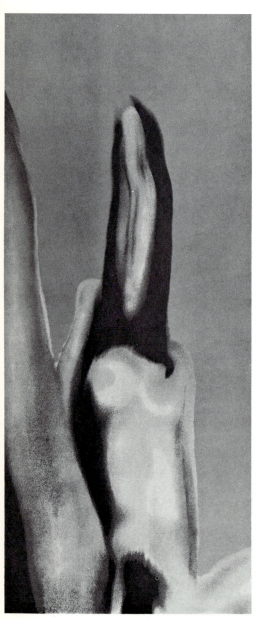

96. Larry Bell. *Untitled #3.* 1974.
Five-color screenprint with tinted varnish
and white rayon flocking,
6′ × 2′6″ (1.83 × .76 m).
Courtesy Graphicstudio,
University of South Florida, Tampa.

table, the process can be repeated for every sheet of paper and every subsequent color.

This method is more time consuming than using register stops, but when care is taken not to move the paper once it has been positioned, it is extremely accurate. A vacuum table is a great help in holding the paper firmly in place.

Flocked Prints

A *flocked* print is made by printing with an adhesive varnish. While the varnish is still tacky, fibers, tinsel, pearl flakes, or other materials can be applied to give the print a glittery, suedelike, velvety, or textured effect. The technique has been used commercially for decades. Some artists have made use of its tactile and sensory qualities to great advantage in contemporary printmaking (Fig. 96).

Before the area can be flocked, it must first be screenprinted with adhesive, which dries to a slightly yellow tint. (This adhesive can be purchased in a variety of colors or can be tinted with inks.) Flocking material is available in different colors and should be applied to the image shortly after the adhesive has been screened on. Place each print in a cardboard box slightly larger than the paper, and dust handfuls of flock onto the image areas. Leave the prints in a drying rack for a minimum of 8 hours, making sure that nothing touches the surfaces.

When the adhesive has dried, there are two methods for removing any remaining excess flock. A soft wallpaper brush with long bristles can be used to gently sweep it off, but this should be done only once. Another technique, helpful for rayon flocking, is to pass an electrostatic gun or wand over the flock, which causes it to stand straight up and results in a softer looking print. (Electrostatic guns can be purchased from most screenprinting supply sources.) Use extreme care in storing flocked prints, for the flocking can be damaged quite easily.

Cleaning the Screen

After all printing has been completed, the screen and the other equipment must be cleaned thoroughly. Place several sheets of newspaper onto the printing surface, and lower the screen on top. Scrape excess ink from the screen's edges and store the ink in a container for future use. Scrape the excess ink from the squeegee blade, and then clean it with solvent. Make sure the blade and the wooden handle are spotless.

Pour a small amount of appropriate solvent (kerosene, mineral spirits, paint thinner, or turpentine) directly onto the screen. Clean the ink from the screen by wiping the solvent around the inside of the frame and over the image with rags (Fig. 97). Replace the newsprint often with fresh sheets until most of the ink has been removed. Lift up the screen, and with two clean rags and some additional solvent, rub both sides of the screen simultaneously, working until the printing areas appear immaculate when held up to the light. If the screen is to be reused, be careful not to damage the stencil on the bottom. Place all used rags in a fireproof metal container and empty the container frequently. Never leave them lying about because they create a fire hazard.

Removing Direct Emulsion

After printing, the ink is removed first from the screen with solvent, followed by the direct photo emulsion, which then can be removed easily with a solution of equal parts of water and ordinary household bleach. (Silk cannot be reclaimed this way, because the bleach destroys the fabric, but nylon and polyester are unaffected by bleach and can be reclaimed many times.)

Apply the solution to both sides of the screen to soften the emulsion. Next, scrub the emulsion off with a nylon bristle brush, and spray the screen with hot water.

Removing Presensitized Film

If you have used the indirect photo method for making the stencil, remove as much of the printing ink from the screen as possible, using lacquer thinner to remove stubborn particles of oil, cellulose, or enamel inks. Spray the presensitized film with hot water from both sides of the screen, then scrub with a nylon brush on both sides

97. Cleaning ink from the screen with rags and solvent.

of the fabric (Figs. 98, 99). If it is difficult to remove the film completely, use an enzyme stencil remover. (Any screenprinting supply source will carry one.) Finally, the screen should be rinsed with a 5-percent solution of acetic acid or with vinegar to kill any active enzymes remaining in the fabric. Then, rinse the screen with clean water.

Removing Lacquer Film

After printing, wash the ink thoroughly from the screen. Then remove the film and blockout solution with lacquer thinner. Make sure that your work space is well ventilated because lacquer thinner fumes are noxious and highly flammable.

A good procedure for cleaning is to place several thicknesses of newspaper under the screen on a flat table and pour some thinner on the screen, allowing it to set for a minute or so. Rub the top of the screen lightly with a cloth or paper towels, then lift the screen. A good portion of the film and the blockout solution will be left on the newspaper. Change the papers and repeat until the screen is clean.

For a final cleaning, hold the screen vertically, and rub both sides of it simultaneously with two cloths wet with lacquer thinner. Check frequently to see if any ink or blockout still remains in the screen by holding it up to a light, and repeat if necessary.

Self-Containing Tray

To avoid the need for a large tray to soak the screen in solvent during the cleaning process, vinyl or a similar plastic can be placed under the screen and taped to the top of the wood frame (Fig. 100). Solvents may be poured on the screen and allowed to stand for extended periods for removal of stubborn stains and ink. Test the plastic first to be sure that it will be unaffected by the solvent used. Vinyl plastic will dissolve in lacquer thinner and in other solvents. However, Mylar is unaffected by these solvents. Most plastics are unaffected by bleach; therefore, the self-containing tray is very useful for softening direct photo emulsion with bleach (Clorox) prior to cleaning with a hose or power spray.

left: 98. Presensitized film is removed with hot water.

right: 99. The screen should then be scrubbed with a nylon brush.

100. Plastic taped around
the bottom of the screen frame
makes a self-contained tray
to hold solvents used for cleaning.

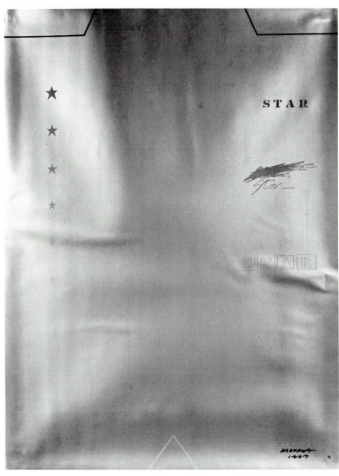

101. Arakawa. *Untitled* (*Star*). 1967.
Screenprint on Mylar,
46 × 35″ (115 × 87 cm).
Courtesy Multiples, Inc., New York.

Prints Made with Plastics

The first plastics—developed in 1868—were made from cellulose nitrate. The term "plastic" now encompasses a wide range of materials, made up of various combinations of carbon, oxygen, hydrogen, chlorine, fluorine, and nitrogen. First employed for artistic purposes in unique works by Naum Gabo, Antoine Pevsner, and the Bauhaus artists László Moholy-Nagy and Gyorgy Kepes, plastics—particularly acrylic—soon became popular art materials. By the end of World War II, plastics technology had become readily available to artists through the widespread use of plastics in advertising and industry.

Plastics fall into two groups—*thermoplastics,* which become soft and malleable in the presence of sufficient heat, and *thermal-setting plastics,* which change irreversibly from liquid to solid when a thermo reaction takes place. Plastics can be reflective (Fig. 101), transparent, translucent, or opaque and are castable.

Acrylic

Because of its dimensional stability, light weight, and ease of fabrication, acrylic sheet offers a great range of potential uses. Working with acrylic is no more complex than working with wood, provided that certain minor modifications are taken into account to accommodate the intrinsic properties of the material (Figs. 102, 103).

Cutting   Acrylic sheets up to approximately $\frac{1}{16}$ inch thick can be scored with a razor blade and snapped apart. Acrylic film for edition printing can be die-cut on a stamp press. For cutting thicker sheets with a table, radial, or panel saw, a standard wood veneer blade usually will suffice. This type of blade reduces chipping and cracking. Do not set blade height more than $\frac{1}{4}$ inch above the material. Because of its thermoplastic properties, acrylic should be cut slowly to avoid melting. When smooth cuts are desired in thick acrylic sheet, a 10 percent solution of soluble oil and water should be applied to the blade during cutting. With a band saw, use a skip-tooth or buttress blade, which has extra gullet capacity and allows for large chips. (Six teeth per inch of blade is the recommended size.) When cutting with a saber saw, use a nonferrous metal blade of fourteen to sixteen teeth per inch. A Cutawl with a #22 blade can cut intricate shapes, provided it is moved slowly across the surface of the plastic.

Drilling   Acrylic can be drilled in the same manner as wood and metal. The tip of the bit, however, should have a 60-degree bevel, with a dubbed-off area at the cutting point. These drill bits are easy to obtain. Drilling should be done at the highest possible speed (approximately 5000 RPM). For large holes (greater than $\frac{1}{2}$ inch), reduce the speed to 1000 RPM. In *Mirage Morning* (Fig. 104) James Rosenquist drilled through acrylic sheet and riveted window shade hardware to its surface.

Sanding and Polishing   Machined surfaces can be restored to their original smooth and highly polished state by a progressive-step sanding procedure, beginning with No. 120 grit and advancing to

left: 102. The edge of an acrylic sheet can be polished by a controlled flame. The protective backing has been rolled back here.

right: 103. A shaped piece of acrylic is laminated to a rectangular acrylic sheet by means of solvent applied with a hypodermic needle.

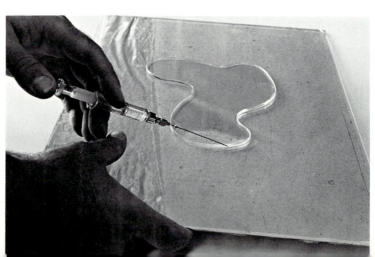

240, 320, and finally 400. It is preferable to wet the acrylic while sanding. After the sanding has been completed, the acrylic can be restored to its original surface by polishing with a polishing wheel and alumina abrasive. A final polishing should be done on a clean soft buffing wheel without compound. Sanding and buffing are recommended as preliminary steps to solvent cementing and gluing. An edge-polishing technique is flame polishing, in which an oxygen-hydrogen flame is passed quickly over the edge. (Carbon-base fuel should not be used.)

Gluing   Commercially available methylene chloride generally is used for solvent cementing of acrylic sheet, either by direct application or through capillary action. This solvent cement is applied with a hypodermic needle or a fine brush along the seam. Other adhesives, such as epoxy, also can be used, but these do not fuse the material together, and they require a rough surface to be effective.

Care and Cleaning   Acrylic sheet normally has a negative polarity, which makes it attract particles in the air. To neutralize this electrostatic effect, the surface should be cleaned with isopropyl alcohol and a soft cloth. To remove minute scratches, buff with a surface finish polish such as Mirror-glaze compound.

Placing Images on Acrylic Sheet   The most common ways of placing an image on acrylic are brushing, spraying, and screening. Before screening an image, clean the acrylic with isopropyl alcohol in the manner described above. Screening should take place at 70 percent humidity or below, to guarantee permanent adhesion of the paint. If *vacuum forming* (see p. 111) is to take place, a flexible paint product (such as Grip-Flex FR-1) should be used for screening.

105. Larry Rivers.
French Money. 1965.
Screenprint on acrylic
with acrylic collage,
32 × 30″ (80 × 75 cm).
Courtesy Multiples, Inc., New York.

Larry Rivers' *French Money* (Fig. 105) is an example of a screened image on acrylic, with the addition of smaller, shaped acrylic forms that have been solvent cemented to the surface. In Robert Rauschenberg's *Star Quarters* (Pl. 9, p. 94), produced at Styria Studios in New York, acrylic sheet was screened on both sides and then vacuum plated with a mirror surface on the back (Figs. 106, 107). The fact that the sheet could be printed on both sides provided a physical space to juxtapose the images, which in turn were compounded by the reflexive surface of the mirror.

Forming Thermoplastics

The technique of forming thermoplastics is fundamentally the same for acrylic, vinyl, urethane, styrene, and polyethylene. The two

left: 106. Because of the thickness of the acrylic, acrylic stops are glued to the table as a registration device.

right: 107. After the final run the screen is lifted from the acrylic surface.

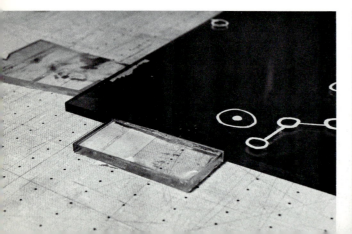

processes that offer the greatest potential for expanding the range of graphic images are *vacuum forming* and *press molding.* In both cases, the material must be brought to its moldable temperature by infrared lamps, heating coil, or a commercially available oven.

Vacuum Forming and Printing   Plastic sheeting can be vacuum-formed over any object—within its stretching limitations—to produce high-fidelity reproductions of that object. This is accomplished by placing the object on a vacuum table, draping plastic over it, heating the plastic, and withdrawing the air so that the plastic is sucked down toward the table and around the object. Commercially available machines, like those manufactured by Plasti-Vac, Incorporated, are ideal. You also can build a vacuum-forming machine with a vacuum cleaner or a vacuum pump connected to a drilled Formica-on-plywood table top (Fig. 108).

If the object over which the plastic is being formed extends over the holes in the vacuum table, a small spacer should be used between the object and the table. If the object is placed on a piece of wood (Fig. 109), cut ridges in the back of the wood from the vacuum hole to the holes under the edge of the object. To ensure the sealing effect necessary to draw a vacuum, the plastic sheet can be mounted to a plywood frame with an interior window cut to the desired dimensions of the finished piece (Fig. 110). Screws or staples

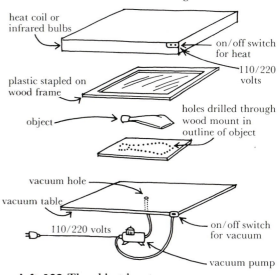

108. A vacuum-forming machine.

heat coil or infrared bulbs

on/off switch for heat

110/220 volts

plastic stapled on wood frame

object

holes drilled through wood mount in outline of object

vacuum hole

vacuum table

110/220 volts

on/off switch for vacuum

vacuum pump

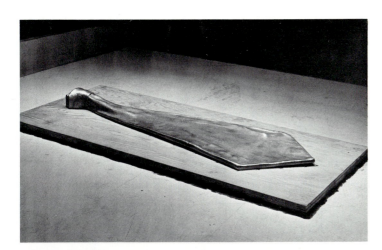

above left: 109. The object is set on a piece of wood with holes drilled along the outline. The wood is wax-sealed to the vacuum table.

left: 110. The wooden frame is held firmly against the object until the plastic is drawn down by the vacuum.

Prints Made with Plastics   **111**

can be used to secure the plastic to the frame. (Drill plastic before using screws to avoid cracking or splitting.) Since the plastic shrinks while cooling, it should be removed from the object as soon as it falls below the thermal-forming temperature (Fig. 111). (To check the draw of the vacuum, pass a lighted match over the vacuum holes. The flame should be sucked down to the holes if the vacuum is working properly.) Claes Oldenburg's *Teabag* is an example of a vacuum-formed object (Fig. 112). Color was screened onto the acrylic backing sheet and the felt teabag. The bag was then sandwiched between the formed sheet and the backing sheet.

A variation of vacuum forming can be seen in Tom Wesselmann's *Cut Out Nude,* in which *blow forming* was used (Fig. 113). After the images were screened with flexible ink, the plastic was placed over a negative mold and blown down by air pressure.

Press Molding   Press molding is done by heating the plastic until it is pliable, clamping it to a negative mold and pressing a positive mold into it (Fig. 114). James Rosenquist employed this technique for *Earth and Moon* in order to form the outer sheet of the hourglass, which then was trimmed and glued to a backing sheet (Fig. 115).

above: 111. The completed vacuum-formed image of styrene plastic should be removed from the original as it begins to cool.

right: 112. Claes Oldenburg. *Teabag.* 1966. Screenprint on felt, Plexiglas, and plastic, with felt bag and rayon cord attached; $39\frac{3}{8} \times 28\frac{1}{8} \times 3''$ ($98 \times 70 \times 7$ cm). Museum of Modern Art, New York (gift of Lester Avnet).

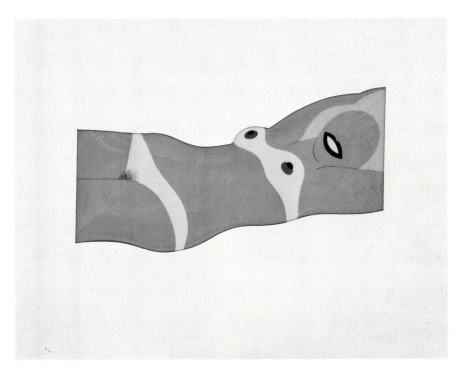

113. Tom Wesselmann.
Cut Out Nude. 1965.
Serigraph on vacuum-formed plastic,
$7\frac{7}{8} \times 16\frac{1}{4}''$ (19 × 41 cm).
Museum of Modern Art, New York
(gift of Original Editions).

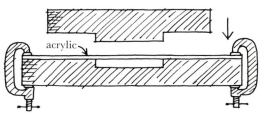

acrylic

above: 114. A sheet of plastic
is clamped to a negative mold,
heated, and press molded
by the positive mold.

right: 115. James Rosenquist.
Earth and Moon. 1971.
Lithograph with Plexiglas hourglass face,
$18\frac{1}{2} \times 17\frac{1}{2}''$ (46 × 44 cm).
Courtesy Graphicstudio,
University of South Florida, Tampa.

Screenprinting on Ceramics, Metal, or Glass

Screenprinting on ceramics, metal, or glass can be accomplished by directly printing a glaze on an object, or by printing on a decal (decalcomania) and transferring the image to the ceramic ware, metal, or glass surface. Once fired, the image will fuse to the object on which it has been placed, creating a durable surface.

Printing on Ceramics

Using a screen (approximately 12XX) which has been prepared with any compatible blockout (photo or hand drawn), ceramic inks (glazes) may be applied to a ceramic object. A frit, or prefired glass mixture (commercially available), can be mixed with underglaze varnish or process printing lacquer as a vehicle. If lacquer is used, $\frac{1}{2}$ ounce of oil of cloves is added to 1 pint of printing lacquer. To this compound butyl lactate is added until the consistency is proper for printing. The oil of cloves reduces the blistering and pinholing of the fired glaze.

Squeegee ceramic material through the screen directly onto a moist clay surface. This glaze material should be ground to a particle size smaller than the screen. A ball mill may be used but requires many hours; finely ground materials are commercially available. The longevity of the screen can be prolonged if oil-base pigments or glazes are used. The following are two such mixtures:

1. 2 parts pigment or glaze
   3 parts varnish (dammar)

2. 1 part varnish (dammar)
   1 part turpentine
   1 part boiled linseed oil

Add pigment to this mixture in a ratio of 2:3 or until the material has the consistency of tube paint.

Best results have been obtained by screening the image onto a smooth, light color mat glaze or engobe surface. The engobe is preferable since its rougher texture contributes to a more integrated union of the image and ceramic object when fired. Further, if you wish to distort or fragment the image, this is best done while the clay is soft.

The following is an engobe for high fire:

1 part volcanic ash
1 part EPK (kaolin)
1 part strontium carbonate

A white porcelain clay firing to cone 10 (2500°F) makes an excellent background:

40% kaolin
10% ball clay
28% feldspar
20% flint
 2% whiting

In Figures 116, 117, and 118, 1 percent cobalt carbonate was added to frit #441 to make a dark blue image. Figure 118 shows the completed work after the bisque firing and clear overglaze firing at cone 06. The dark screening slip into which this was added was:

15% nepheline syenite
85% Albany slip

Low-fire work could be done on white clay such as CT-3 casting and modeling clay from Ex-Cel. You should use low-fire glazes

above left: 116. The image for Charles Fager's *Catenary* is screened on fresh rolled moist clay with black underglaze.

above right: 117. The hand-thrown pots are placed in the kiln.

left: 118. Charles Fager. *Catenary.* 1978. Fired ceramic with silkscreen decoration, 11 × 12 × 6″ (28 × 30 × 15 cm). Courtesy the artist.

119. Clay object for Robert Rauschenberg's *Tampa Clay Piece 3* is removed from the mold at Graphicstudio, University of South Florida, Tampa. (See Fig. 121.)

120. The serigraph decal image is slipped from its backing paper and adhered to the clay.

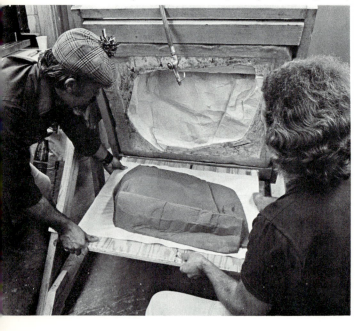

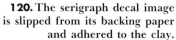
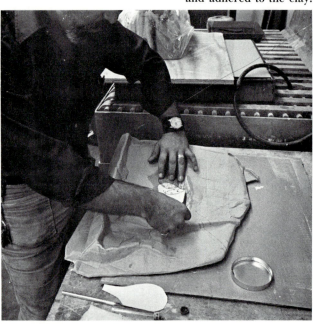

121. Robert Rauschenberg. *Tampa Clay Piece 3.* 1972–73. Press molded with clay silkscreened ceramic glaze, decal, platinum luster glaze, patina, and tape; 19½ × 24 × 5½″ (49 × 60 × 14 cm). Courtesy Graphicstudio, University of South Florida, Tampa.

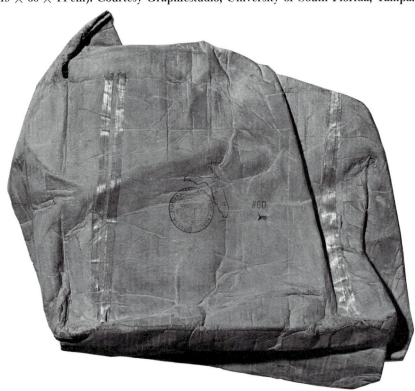

and underglazes such as those available from Duncan, Drakenfeld, or Reward for this process.

Decal Transfer for Ceramics

Working with Alan Eaker, Robert Rauschenberg created a series of press-molded ceramic sculptures at Graphicstudio. These works, editioned by Julio Juristo, utilize silkscreen decal transfers that were fired onto the clay surface. The decal transfer was made in the following way.

A clay piece made from a plaster mold was fired (Fig. 119). Then a piece of decal paper was flood-coated with underglaze varnish through an open silkscreen. Color glazing oxides then were mixed with underglaze varnish and squeegeed through the image screen onto the flood-coated paper. When it had dried, the decal paper was immersed in warm water. In the meantime, the area of the ceramic that was to receive the decal was painted with cellulose gum. The decal, which had been loosened from its backing paper by the water, was slipped off the paper onto the wet cellulose gum and allowed to dry (Fig. 120). The clay, already fired to cone 9, was then fired to cone 06, permanently fixing the decal image to the surface (Fig. 121). Firing the luster glazes at a lower temperature (cone 018) did not alter the decal transfer image. The use of cellulose gum was critical, since other adhesives that were tested bubbled through the image, permanently destroying the work. (For information on coloring oxides and firing procedures, a ceramics manual should always be consulted.)

Printing on Glass

Ceramic glass enamels are fired from 1000 to 1250°F. Colors are commercially available in mat or gloss and transparent or opaque and may be overprinted without individual firing.

Printing on Metal

Porcelain enamel is used for printing on metal. It is an inorganic compound of frit (silica, feldspar, and sand with borax as a flux) and metal. This glasslike material is screened onto a metal surface that has been degreased with a mild acid. The frit and metal (porcelain) is mixed with a vehicle. Kiln-firing temperature should be raised slowly to allow the organic vehicle to burn out. The firing range varies depending upon the thickness of the glaze and the supporting surface; generally it would be in the 1200 to 1600°F range.

SEVEN

Papers for Screenprinting

A great variety of papers produce excellent results in screenprinting. Smooth finishes yield the sharpest possible prints and reproduce the finest detail, although textured sheets are suitable for some applications and can be smoothed somewhat by being run through a litho press between sheets of newsprint. Many types of bristol board, cover stock, and other heavy papers can be used for proofing as well as for printing posters and limited editions. When quality and permanency are desired, heavy Oriental papers and etching and lithography papers serve quite well. Arches 88, a special 100 percent cotton fiber paper, has a smooth finish designed for quality screenprinting. It is available in sheets and in rolls. Rives BFK yields excellent luminosity in transparent overlays of color because of its quality of brightness.

Experimental uses of paper in screenprinting include Alan Shields' *Sun, Moon, Title Page* (Pl. 8, p. 93), a two-sided work on dyed, stitched, and woven paper.

Handmade paper can have a rough or smooth surface, depending on the quality of the beaten pulp, the texture of the felt, and the fineness of the screen. For a smoother finish, the paper is run through a series of polished metal rollers that compress it in varying degrees, depending on the number of times it passes between the rollers and the amount of pressure used. For *hot-pressed papers,* characterized by very smooth surfaces, the polished rollers are heated before the paper is run through. *Cold-pressed papers* can vary in finish from rough to smooth.

Calendered paper serves for certain commercial applications. Calendering is used only for machine-made papers, and produces an extremely smooth, sometimes glossy surface. The web of paper passes through a vertical stack of polished cast iron rollers that crush the fibers to minute tolerances in thickness and thus smooth the paper's surface.

Since the early 13th century Europe always has been a leading supplier of rag papers suitable for printmaking. Although the greatest quantities and varieties of handmade and moldmade papers are still being manufactured in Italy, Germany, Great Britain, and Holland, printmaking papers can now be purchased from mills in the United States. The European techniques of making paper by hand were brought to the United States early, with the establishment of the Rittenhouse Mill in Germantown, Pennsylvania, in 1690. Much later, in 1928, Dard Hunter began operations at Limerock, Connecticut.

More recently, and largely through the persistent efforts of Douglas Howell, a resurgence in the art of hand papermaking has contributed to the development and success of several new operations. In addition to Howell, Aris Koutroulis, Laurence Barker, John and Kathleen Koller, and Kathryn and Howard Clark have helped to keep the tradition alive. Twinrocker, a small mill begun by the Clarks in Indiana, and Handmade Papers, operated by the Kollers in Connecticut, make papers of excellent quality that are used increasingly by printmakers (Fig. 122). Through these independent sources, paper of almost any weight, color, and size can be purchased in small or large quantities.

The standard papers from large European or American mills are available in specific weights and formats. The weights of European papers are always given in grams per square meter. Arches Cover and Rives BFK in the most popular sizes, for example, each weigh 250 grams per square meter. The weight of American-made papers is usually but not always indicated by pounds per ream (five hundred sheets). A cover stock similar in weight to Arches or Rives BFK would weigh approximately 140 pounds per ream. Weight is sometimes expressed in terms of pounds per one thousand sheets—for example, 250 M means 250 pounds per thousand sheets. These weights are not based on standard-size sheets, but on the particular size of the sheet being weighed.

Following is a descriptive list of some of the best papers available from the large commercial mills. Along with the large variety of handmade papers available from small mills, these provide an almost inexhaustible source of good printing papers for the individual screenprinter or for a large studio.

Acta Paper Fabric   A heavyweight paper (approximately 140 pound) of pure alpha cellulose fibers, Acta Paper Fabric is suitable for any technique, and can be embossed, formed, shaped, drawn on,

or printed on with excellent results. It has a medium-smooth, cold-pressed surface and is available in sheets 18 by 24 inches and 24 by 36 inches.

American Etching Machine made from 100 percent rag fibers, American Etching is a relatively soft, off-white, 360-gram paper excellent for etching. This paper also serves well for screenprinting. It is available in 38-by-50-inch sheets.

Apta A beautiful 100 percent rag sheet with a character of its own, Apta is handmade at the Richard de Bas mill in Ambert (Puy-de-Dôme), France. This heavyweight (240 grams), white paper has two watermarks—*Auvergne à la main* in one corner, and *1326,* a heart, and *Richard de Bas* in the other. It is excellent for screenprinting, and comes in sheets 20 by 26 inches.

Aquabee Another 100 percent rag paper is the American-made Aquabee. Its white, very smooth surface is excellent for lithography, screenprinting, and drawing. Aquabee is machine-made in sheets 18 by 24 inches and 24 by 36 inches, as well as in rolls 42 inches wide.

Arches Cover Arches Cover is a beautiful, mold-made, watermarked French paper available in off-white and a warm buff color. This paper has natural deckles on its long edges; the short edges are torn to simulate a deckle. It is 100 percent rag and versatile enough to print not only screenprints, but also etchings and lithographs.

Arches Cover holds color very well, and is better suited for color printing than other papers. It also erases well, making corrections easier. Available in France in a dozen sizes, it can be obtained readily in the United States and Canada in these sizes: 19 by 26 inches, 22 by 30 inches, and 29 by 41 inches. Other sheet sizes and rolls are available on special order from the Arjomari mill in France. Arches Cover weighs 250 grams per square meter.

Arches En-Tout-Cas   A 25 percent rag paper excellent for proofing most types of prints, Arches En-Tout-Cas is also a good student paper for drawing and watercolor work. It weighs 280 grams, is fairly inexpensive, and comes in rolls 52 inches wide by 10 yards long.

Arches Silkscreen   Also known as Arches 88, Arches Silkscreen is 100 percent rag with a very smooth finish. Designed for quality printing in silkscreen work, this paper also prints lithographs and etchings equally well. It is available from Arjomari in rolls, and from domestic suppliers in sheets 22 by 30 inches. Arches Silkscreen is made in two weights, 300 grams and 350 grams.

Arches Text   A fine paper with a laid or wove finish, Arches Text stretches when dampened, and can wrinkle easily unless covered quickly with a blotter and a weight. This paper is excellent for screenprinting. Arches Text is available in sheets 20 by $25\frac{1}{2}$ inches and $25\frac{1}{2}$ inches by 40 inches, the latter size weighing 80 pounds per ream.

Basingwerk   Basingwerk is a dense, very smooth, and comparatively thin English paper made from Esparto grass. Inexpensive, stable, and permanent, it makes an excellent printing and proofing paper for screenprinting, as well as etchings, lithographs, and relief prints. Basingwerk is off-white and comes in two weights, heavy (155 grams) and light (120 grams). Sheets are 26 by 40 inches.

Bodleian   Bodleian is a printing paper excellent for limited edition fine arts books. It is handmade in England of 100 percent rag fibers, weighs 55 grams per square meter, and can be obtained in sheets 20 by 28 inches.

Charter Oak   A beautiful, 100 percent rag paper from the Barcham Green mill in England, Charter Oak is excellent for screenprinting. It is sized and watermarked, weighs 100 grams per square meter, and is made by hand in sheets 20 by 25 inches.

Copperplate   Copperplate, a moldmade paper from Germany, contains little or no sizing. This paper is soft and white and is suitable for screenprinting. It is 34 percent rag and 66 percent high alpha, and has two natural deckles, two torn deckles, and no watermark. Because the edges have a tendency to curl, positioning and registration could prove to be a problem. Copperplate Deluxe exhibits the same characteristic. Copperplate is available in sizes 22 by 30 inches and 30 by 42½ inches, and weighs 250 grams per square meter.

Copperplate Deluxe   Similar to Copperplate in weight and appearance, Copperplate Deluxe is composed of 75 percent rag and 25 percent high alpha. Its absorbent surface is excellent for multiple overlays of color, although its curled edges create a problem in registration. Heavy pressure and heavy inking yield the best results on Copperplate Deluxe. While it is best for etching, lithography, collagraph prints, and embossing, this paper can be used for screenprinting. It comes in sheets 22 by 30 inches and 30 by 42½ inches, the latter size weighing 220 pounds per ream. Copperplate Deluxe is produced by Papierfabrik Zerkall, Germany.

Crisbrook   Crisbrook is a fine, 100 percent rag, white waterleaf paper from the Barcham Green mill in England. It is 140-pound, unsized, hot pressed, and watermarked. Excellent for detailed work of all kinds, Crisbrook has good luminosity for color work, although the ink may have to be modified in order to prevent glossing when overprinting. The sheets are 22 by 30 inches.

De Wint   Another Barcham Green paper, De Wint is tinted brown and made of 100 percent rag. It is sized but useful for all techniques, and is made in 22½-by-30-inch and 30-by-44-inch sheets. Its weight per square meter is 300 grams.

German Etching   German Etching paper is similar in many respects to Copperplate Deluxe. This high-quality, 300-gram off-white paper is suitable for the various printing techniques. German Etching is composed of 100 percent rag. It has two natural deckles and two torn deckles, and comes in 22-by-30-inch and 30-by-42-inch sheets. The 30-by-42-inch sheet also is available in black. German Etching paper is manufactured by Buettenpapierfabrik, which is located in Germany.

Hayle   A handmade, 110-gram paper from the Barcham Green mill, Hayle is useful for small deluxe editions. This 100 percent rag paper is excellent for screenprinting. Hayle is made on a laid screen and watermarked, with four natural deckles, and is available in a 15½-by-20½-inch sheet.

Ingres Antique   Ingres Antique is an Italian laid paper available in white and eight colors. It is suitable for most printmaking techniques, as well as for calligraphy and drawing. The weight of this paper is 95 grams per square meter; sheets are $18\frac{3}{4}$ by $24\frac{3}{4}$ inches in size.

Italia   A beautiful, bright white paper, Italia is heavy, dense, quite soft, and an ideal choice for single-color work of all kinds. Composed of 50 percent rag and 50 percent high alpha, this paper absorbs very little ink. Italia is an excellent paper for screenprinting. It occasionally has surface imperfections, and the texture is variable. The paper is watermarked and available in 20-by-28-inch and 28-by-40-inch sizes. The larger size has two natural deckles on the long sides and torn deckles on the short sides; the smaller sheets are torn from the larger ones. Italia is made by Cartiere Enrico Magnani Mill, located in Pescia, Italy. Large sheets weigh 260 pounds per ream.

J. Barcham Green   A moldmade, 100 percent rag paper available in rough, cold-pressed, or hot-pressed finishes, J. Barcham Green is made by the English mill of the same name. This warm white paper is unsized, smooth, and 140 pound. In addition to watercolor work—for which it was designed—J. Barcham Green is excellent for screenprinting. It takes detail and color quite well and is available in 22-by-30-inch sheets. Another weight, 133 pound, is also available in sheets 26 by 40 inches.

Johannot   A product of the Arjomari mill in France, Johannot is a watermarked paper with two natural and two torn deckles. Moldmade of 100 percent rag, with a slightly textured finish, this paper is well suited for screenprinting. Sheets are 22 by 30 inches and 20 by 41 inches. Johannot is made in two weights, 125 grams and 240 grams.

Lenox 100   Lenox 100, or Lenox Cover, is an excellent American paper suitable for all techniques, especially screenprinting. It is white, smooth surfaced, 100 percent rag with a neutral pH and comes in 115-, 180-, and 330-pound weights. Moldmade, with two natural and two torn deckles, Lenox 100 is also available in several sizes: $17\frac{1}{2}$ by 23 inches, 22 by 30 inches, 26 by 40 inches, and 38 by 50 inches.

Lenox 25   A proofing paper most helpful for any printing technique, Lenox 25 is very similar to Lenox 100 in color and texture, although it is only 25 percent rag. Its weight is 190 grams per square meter, and the sheets are 25 by 38 inches.

Murillo   A heavy (360 grams), cream-colored paper with a textured surface, Murillo may be used for screenprinting. This paper is 25 percent rag. It is available from the Fabriano mill in Italy and also comes in black. The sheets are $27\frac{1}{2}$ by $39\frac{1}{2}$ inches.

Opaline Parchment   An extremely smooth-textured and translucent Swiss paper, Opaline Parchment is particularly useful for calligraphy as well as for screenprinting. Its weight is 160 grams; the sheets are 22 by 28½ inches.

Rives BFK   A very white, moldmade paper of 100 percent rag fibers, Rives BFK is made by the Arjomari mill in France. This paper is normally very lightly sized, but on special orders the sizing can be increased. It is an excellent choice for screenprinting. Rives BFK is watermarked, with two natural and two torn deckles, and is available in sheets 19 by 26 inches, 22 by 30 inches (weighing 240 grams per square meter), and 29 by 41 inches (weighing 260 grams per square meter). This paper also can be found unsized in rolls 42 inches by 100 yards.

Rives Velin Cuve Teinte Papier (BFK Gray)   A beautifully toned, gray-buff paper similar in color to newsprint, Rives Velin Cuve Teinte Papier is 100 percent rag, available in sheets 30 by 40 inches. It weighs 260 grams per square meter.

Rives BFK Papier de Lin   A new Rives paper made of 25 percent linen rag and 75 percent cotton, Papier de Lin is heavyweight (270 grams per square meter) with either a rough or a cold-pressed finish. It is suitable for screenprinting and is highly stable and durable. The sheets are 22 by 30 inches.

Rives Lightweight and Rives Heavyweight   Two 100 percent rag papers, Rives Lightweight (115 grams) and Rives Heavyweight (175 grams) are both lighter than Rives BFK. They are moldmade in buff and off-white, and watermarked, with two natural and two torn deckles. Both of these quality papers serve beautifully for screenprinting.

Roma   Roma is a beautiful, 100 percent rag, handmade Italian paper. Light to medium in weight, it has a medium sizing. It has limited absorbency for color printing, however, and if an image is printed to the edge of the sheet, the watermark may show. Roma is available in eight colors and is easy to obtain in 19-by-26-inch sheets. Other sizes for large quantity orders can be supplied by the Fabriano mill. This paper weighs 130 grams per square meter.

Strathmore Artist Bristol   An American-made paper of 100 percent cotton rag, Strathmore Artist Bristol is available in smooth or shiny finishes, and in 1-, 2-, 3-, 4-, or 5-ply weights. (Multiple-ply weights will separate if dampened.) This paper is not watermarked, but it has an embossed chop on one corner and is most useful for screenprinting. It is available in 23-by-29-inch sheets and 30-by-40-inch sheets.

Tableau   A white paper with a strong, long-fibered texture, Tableau is a vegetable parchment made from hemp, and serves well for various printmaking techniques. It resembles certain Japanese papers and can also be used for interleaving. This paper is made in 18-by-24-inch and 24-by-36-inch sheets, and in 40-inch rolls 60 and 160 feet long. The 24-by-36-inch sheets weigh 21 pounds per ream. The paper is available in heavier weights. The heavier papers can be used for screenprinting.

Tovil   A beautiful, fully deckled, cream-colored sheet, Tovil is handmade of 100 percent rag in a medium weight (110 grams). It has two strong watermarks and fairly hard sizing, and is excellent for screenprinting. Each sheet is $15\frac{1}{2}$ by $20\frac{1}{2}$ inches.

Umbria   Umbria shares many of the characteristics of Roma and is made by the same mill. This soft, handmade paper of 100 percent rag fibers serves well for all techniques. It is a watermarked, slightly sized 60-pound paper available in 20-by-26-inch sheets.

Wood Pulp Papers

Contemporary production of paper from wood pulp has been vastly improved since the first large-scale utilization of wood for pulp in the mid-1800s. The 19th-century method employed sodium hydroxide, which broke down the cellulose fibers of the wood and separated them from the lignin, pectins, and carbohydrates. This resulted in a relatively weak, short-fibered paper. In 1884, a new process in which calcium or magnesium bisulphite was the active ingredient resulted in a longer and therefore stronger fiber. This became known as the *sulphite process*. Sodium sulphate was later added in the course of what is essentially the earlier soda method, resulting in a strong sulphate pulp. This came to be called *kraft* pulp (from the German word meaning strong) and is used in such products as wrapping papers and adhesive tapes.

Alpha Cellulose   More recently, the production of *alpha cellulose* has had many applications in the paper industry. The alpha cellulose is that portion of the pulp or cellulosic material in the wood that resists solution by sodium hydroxide at ordinary temperatures. It is produced by briefly treating pulp with a 17.5 percent solution of sodium hydroxide at 20°C. Following the initial mercerization and softening of the fibers, the solution is diluted to about 9.5 percent sodium hydroxide, filtered, and washed with 10-percent acetic acid and water to neutralize the alkali. Finally, it is washed again to free the fibers of acid. Alpha fibers are stronger and of greater length than any produced by previous methods. Their natural pH factor also ensures an extremely durable paper— perhaps as durable as the best rag papers.

With improved techniques in methods of making paper from wood cellulose—in particular the development of alpha cellulose fibers—there is no doubt that many better grade commercial papers will be used increasingly for limited fine art editions.

Better-Quality Wood Pulp Paper

The commercial offset papers in the following list are excellent long-lasting wood pulp papers for proofing. Most have cut edges, no deckle, and very smooth or slightly textured surfaces. They are also ideal for screenprinting. Most come in white and various colors.

- Beckett Cover, 20 × 26″, 26 × 40″, 23 × 35″, and 35 × 45″
- Carrara Cover, 23 × 29″ and 26 × 40″
- Classic Cover, 8½ × 13″, 23 × 35″, and 26 × 40″
- Cortlea Cover, 26 × 40″ and 23 × 35″
- Index, 26 × 40″
- Linweave Quality Cover, 20 × 26″, 23 × 35″, and 26 × 40″
- Mohawk Superfine Cover, 20 × 26″ and 26 × 40″
- Mohawk Vellum Cover, 23 × 35″, 26 × 40″, and 35 × 46″
- Navajo Cover, 20 × 26″, 23 × 29″, 23 × 35″, 26 × 40″, and 35 × 46″
- Nekoosa Cover Vellum, 20 × 26″, 26 × 40″, 23 × 35″, and 35 × 45″
- Pericles Cover, partial rag, 26 × 40″
- Tuscan Cover, 26 × 40″
- Weyerhauser Starwhite Cover, 20 × 26″

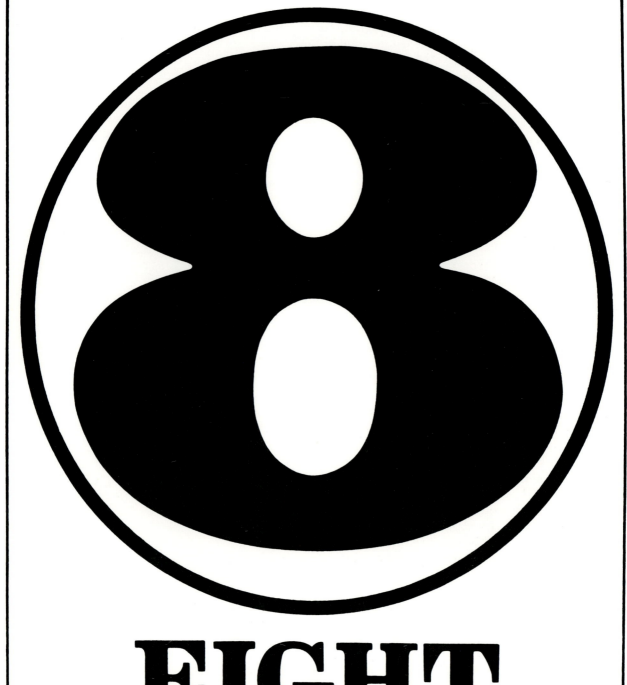

EIGHT

Printing on Textiles

Screenprinting on textiles was uncommon until the mid-1930s. At that time new methods were developed that required less investment in equipment and preparation. The silkscreen, which had already been used for paper printing and some textile printing, quickly found its place, on a small scale, in the textile industry, and, on a much larger scale, in the studios of individual fabric printers.

Screenprinted fabrics have a special color quality known as *bloom*—a less mechanical and often more aesthetically pleasing appearance than fabrics printed by other techniques. The visual and tactile qualities of fabric combined with its receptivity to color make it an exciting and interesting surface for the printmaker to discover and explore.

The creative possibilities of fabric printing are many, in both applied art and fine art forms. Figure 123 shows a repeated pattern print that can be used functionally as material for such individual articles as clothing, bedding, and tablecloths. The wall piece (Fig. 124) shows the application of textile printmaking to create an art object. Both of these one-of-a-kind pieces are statements of personal expression.

This chapter will introduce the beginning fabric printer to the unique qualities of fabric as a printing medium. It presents an overview of dyes and pigments and their properties, and explains basic techniques using readily available materials and equipment.

The Fabric

There are a great variety of available fabrics from which to choose. Each has its own special characteristics such as:

o smoothness—roughness
o sheerness—texture
o shiny surface—mat surface
o loose weave—tight weave
o stretch—stability
o dimension

A finish will affect the receptivity of the fabric to the dyes and pigments used in printing. It is strongly recommended that you not buy fabrics which are marked "stain resistant," "water resistant," or "water repellent."

It is important to know the fiber content of the fabric you are printing. There are basically two categories of fibers: natural and manufactured. Natural fibers can be broken down further into two groups, cellulosic and protein. The natural and manufactured fibers of most interest to printers are listed below.

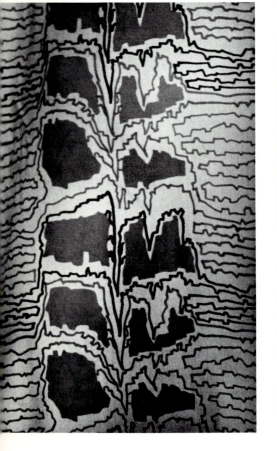

123. Betsy Damos.
Screenprinted fabric from the series *Spectra Prints.* 1977. Polyester and cotton. Courtesy the artist.

Natural		Manufactured
Cellulosic	**Protein**	
cotton	wool	polyester
linen	silk	polyamide
jute		acrylic
		acetate
		triacetate
		viscose rayon

The Printing Media

While they often look the same, the printing media used on fabric differ considerably in composition from those used on paper. The following discussion will refer to the two fabric printing media—pigment print paste and print paste using dye.

Pigments and dyes, in printing, differ mainly in the way they attach themselves to the fabric. For a pigment print paste, the colorant is generally attached with a resin binder to the surface of the fiber by heat fixation. With a dye print paste the colorant enters and is locked within the fiber of the fabric during fixation.

124. Patricia Dreher.
Birth of Venus. 1977.
Mixed fabrics screenprinted, handpainted,
with photo imagery and trapunto.
Courtesy the artist.

Print Paste Using Pigment

Composition:

○ emulsion
○ color concentrate
○ binder

Advantages:

○ Fixation is easily accomplished with dry heat.
○ The original printed color does not change greatly after fixation.
○ The paste is easily available.
○ It is appropriate for use on all fibers.
○ Because it can be made opaque, it offers the possibility of printing a light color on a dark ground.
○ It has a long shelf life.

o It is lightfast.
o It does not require washing after fixing unless you want to produce a softer fabric.

Disadvantages:

o Pigment printing sometimes stiffens the *hand* of the fabric. (Hand refers to the way the fabric feels.) Therefore, pigment is often inappropriate for fabrics with a deep pile or brushed surface (such as corduroy, velvet, velveteen, suede cloth, or terrycloth) since it might leave these fabrics with a stiff hand.
o On very slick or shiny fabrics the pigment print might *crock* (flake or rub off).
o Pigment sometimes tends to dull the look of a shiny fabric such as satin, which can be a disadvantage if you want to maintain this shiny look.

While early pigment pastes required mineral spirits as a solvent for cleanup and as a necessary component in the emulsion, the new improved pigment pastes are water-soluble. The newer pastes offer a number of advantages, particularly in eliminating the noxious fumes of solvents, the possible fire hazards, and the disposal problems. Ecological concerns have also contributed to the development of all-aqueous pigment pastes with little or no solvent additive.

The novice fabric printer should be aware that textile pigment pastes requiring solvent are still on the market. However, the water-soluble pastes are recommended because of their ease of handling and will be the pigment pastes discussed here.

Pigment pastes have traditionally been composed of an emulsion, a color concentrate, and a binder. Depending on the manufacturer, these components are combined in different ways.

Partially prepared pastes for textiles are generally available through large screenprinting supply companies and are known by various trade names, such as Colortex, Fab-Tone, Versatex, and Aqua-Set. Some can also be purchased in art-supply stores and art-school stores. The list of suppliers at the end of this book provides addresses from which these products can be obtained.

Preparing Pigment Print Paste   Most pigment pastes will have a colorless extender base. The extender is used to make a given color lighter. The transparency of a color increases in relation to the amount of extender base added to a pigment concentrate. This is useful in printing one color over another in order to create a third color in the overlapping areas.

Another way of lightening the paste is by the addition of opaque white, which can be used when it is necessary or desirable to print on a darker ground. Because of the high pigment concentration in opaque white, its addition to other colors often has a tendency to stiffen the finished fabric and give the color a chalky look. It is therefore recommended that you use white sparingly, unless it is your intention to achieve these special effects.

Using Pigment Print Pastes   You should always experiment with pigment-extender ratios when first using a new product. The smallest amount of pigment concentrate necessary to achieve a given color value is desirable, both for economic reasons and to produce a fabric with the softest possible hand. However, there is a point at which the addition of too much extender base to the concentrate will affect colorfastness.

When trying out a new color or product you should mix and print a series of shades ranging from darkest value to lightest, using the least amount of pigment necessary to produce the darkest color. These quantities of pigment and extender should be measured carefully by weight or in standard kitchen measure if a scale is not available. Keep good notes directly on a test swatch with indelible marker; heat set the swatch, and wash a portion of each swatch. You will then have an approximate record of the color range available for each hue and an indication of its washability.

Pigment print pastes are relatively easy to mix and to work with directly. They are available in a wide range of premixed colors, which can be intermixed to produce endless variations. Be aware that the paste color in the container will look considerably different from the printed color on the fabric. Colors also change as they dry; generally they become lighter. The color may alter again very slightly after heat setting.

Fixation   After printing, and when the fabric is thoroughly dry, it is necessary to *fix* the print paste permanently to the fabric surface. This is done with dry heat in the range of 285° to 325°F (140–175°C) for 3 to 4 minutes. Temperatures will vary depending on the product, and you should follow the instructions indicated by the manufacturer. The small-scale printer can have considerable success with a dry iron or with a mangle, if available. Some companies suggest using a hot commercial dryer. If the fiber involved necessitates using a lower temperature than that recommended for the print paste, the time should be increased. Be sure fixation takes place evenly in all areas of the fabric. With pigment paste printing it is not necessary to after-wash except to improve the hand.

Print Paste Using Dye

Composition:

o dye
o thickener
o water
o auxiliary chemicals

Advantages:

o Because of the way the dye particles combine with the fiber of the fabric, dyes maintain the original hand of the fabric (for example, the softness of some silk).
o Because the dye does not sit on the surface, a lustrous fabric is not made dull.
o Dyes work well on fabrics that have a deep pile (velvet, velveteen, terrycloth, corduroy) because they will not mat the pile. They will also penetrate these thicker fabrics more easily.

Disadvantages:

o Dyes tend to be more difficult for the beginning printer to work with, because most of the components in the print paste do not come premixed. Some of the necessary chemicals may be difficult to find locally and will have to be obtained directly from mail-order suppliers.
o Products and recommended working methods might differ slightly among manufacturers, making it difficult to standardize printing procedures.
o Fixation of most dyes is more complex than fixation of pigments and may require equipment not readily available at home or in the studio.
o Some dyes contain unstable chemicals, which shorten the shelf life of the dye paste after mixing.
o After fixation washing is necessary to remove unfixed color, thickeners, and residual chemicals.

Classification of Dyes   Dyes are classified in various ways; the most common refers to the method of application. These classifications should not be confused with household dye brand names (such as RIT, Dylon, Tintex) or industrial trade names (such as Procion, Dispersol, or Cibalan).

Some of the most commonly used dyes are: acid, direct, vat, fiber-reactive, and disperse. The table opposite lists some of the descriptive characteristics of each. It must be remembered that these are generalizations. Within a single classification there may be colors that do not have all of the listed properties.

Selecting the Correct Dye   There is at least one appropriate dye for every fiber. When you have a choice, it is wise to examine the advantages and disadvantages of each. For example, silk can be printed with acid dyes or fiber-reactives. Some acid dyes produce more brilliant colors on silk than fiber-reactives; however, generally speaking, acid dyes have a lower washfastness. Fiber-reactives, on the other hand, are highly lightfast and washfast, but may not give as brilliant a color. Therefore, if brilliance is your concern, you should choose acid dyes; if washability, choose fiber-reactives.

Characteristics of Commonly Used Dyes

Acid	Direct
good lightfastness	very good lightfastness
fair to good washfastness	poor to fair washfastness
brilliant color	medium brilliance
suitable for silk, nylon, wool	suitable for cotton, viscose rayon, linen, wool, silk

Vat	Fiber-Reactive
excellent lightfastness	very good lightfastness
excellent washfastness	very good washfastness
brilliant color	brilliant color
quite difficult for beginner to apply	can be fixed by a variety of methods
suitable for cotton, viscose rayon, linen	suitable for cotton (best when mercerized), viscose rayon, linen, wool, silk

Disperse
good lightfastness
good washfastness
brilliant color
sold in powder or paste form
suitable for polyester, Qiana, acetate

Fiber-reactive dyes work best with natural fibers. For manufactured fibers, you may want to print with dye (instead of resin-bonded pigments) to preserve some special fabric qualities. Polyester and cellulose acetate are two manufactured fibers that can be printed with disperse dye. Some of the companies that supply individuals with small quantities of dyes are now offering a group of disperse dyes and printing chemicals.

Preparing Dye Print Paste   Printing with dyestuffs can be thought of as controlled, localized dyeing. Dye powders dissolve in water but must be thickened in order to produce a vehicle suitable for printing. This is achieved by the addition of a thickening agent. The thickening agent holds the dye within the printed area while drying takes place. This thickener must also hold up during the fixation process, and yet must be easily washed out after fixation. If any thickener remains in the finished fabric, the fabric will be stiff in the printed areas.

There are many types of thickening agents available, and the type of dyestuff involved will determine your choice. In some cases there will be a number to select from. Many thickeners, such as gums and starches, are derived from plants and trees. Sodium alginate, a commonly used thickener, is derived from seaweed.

Techniques of printing with dye have been developed and perfected by industry. In industrial printing, dye recipes are usually measured by weight, not volume. A commercial printer will have a color card from the dyestuff manufacturer showing the darkest possible shades of a given color, and also a lighter version. For example, Imperial Chemical Industries (ICI) provides a color card for their fiber-reactive (Procion) dyes that indicates the darkest shades as 4.5 percent mixtures. This means that 4.5 percent of the print paste is dye powder and the other 95.5 percent is thickener, chemicals, and water. Note that very little dye powder is needed to produce a dark color; excess dye will not necessarily increase color value and might create problems.

Since these color cards are not always available to individuals, and since the difficulty of closely controlling variables in a small studio may result in a different dye quantity/color-weight relationship, it is suggested that you produce your own color library. A color card should indicate how much dye was in each print paste, either in percentage or by direct measure. Swatches of fabric should be properly printed, fixed, and washed, and attached to the card.

The Dye Process

It seems appropriate to discuss the dye process—mixing, fixation, and after-wash—in more detail. The emphasis will be placed on fiber-reactive dyes because of their versatility and availability. They also can be applied to a number of fibers and therefore are usually of interest to small-scale printers. Fixation can take place in several ways with equipment that is accessible to most people.

Mixing a Fiber-Reactive Print Paste   The following recipe is based on ICI's formula for a stock thickener, containing all the necessary chemicals without the dyestuff. Quantities are given in both gram and kitchen measure. The desired amount of Procion fiber-reactive powder can be added to this stock paste. The instructions will apply to all fiber-reactive pastes with slight variations.

Calgon is a powdered water softener added since hard water might affect the printing (available in grocery stores). Sodium alginate thickener is known by trade names of Halltex, Manutex, and Keltex. It comes in granular form, and is available in various

Ingredients	Grams	Kitchen Measure*
Calgon	4.5	1 teaspoon
sodium alginate (Halltex KRS-H)	18	4 teaspoons
urea	140	10 tablespoons
protective oxidizing agent (Resist Salt L)	4	1 teaspoon

*Based on an approximate weight-to-volume conversion for each ingredient [1 level teaspoon Procion dye weighs 3 grams; urea, 5 grams; Halltex (dry), 4.5 grams; Resist Salt L, 4 grams; sodium bicarbonate, 5 grams].

viscosities for special printing situations. Urea aids in dissolving dye. It is hygroscopic (absorbs moisture from the air) and therefore attracts moisture in steaming, and comes in crystal form. The protective oxidizing agent is known by trade names of Resist Salt L, Nacan, Ludigol, Sitol; it comes in flakes. Sodium bicarbonate (baking soda) is an alkali instrumental in the chemical reaction between fiber and dye.

Dissolve Calgon in 1½ pints of water; sprinkle in sodium alginate thickener (if using Halltex, use KRS-H), and stir. It may be necessary to let this stand overnight until it is free of lumps. Add urea and protective oxidizing agent, and stir until dissolved. Add enough water to make a quart. This mixture will keep indefinitely if refrigerated in a closed container. It provides all the chemicals necessary for printing except dyestuff and one more very important chemical, sodium bicarbonate. (Sodium bicarbonate is omitted when printing on chlorinated wool or when using a pretreatment with sodium carbonate, which is discussed later.)

The dye powder is made into a pastelike form with a few drops of water (to help it dissolve) and is then added to the stock thickener. The sodium bicarbonate should be added to the print paste just before printing. It is first mixed into a paste with a very small amount of water, then added in the proportion of 1 teaspoon of dry powder per cup of print paste. Stirring is important. Once dye and bicarbonate have been added to a print paste, it will keep a week or so under refrigeration.

If the thickener does not have the proper consistency, you can thicken it by adding slightly more sodium alginate, or thin it by adding more water. If much water has to be added, you should dissolve urea in the water in the proportion of 3 tablespoons of urea for every cup of water.

If you want a vehicle for painting directly on the fabric, you can make it by following the directions above, but adding less alginate for a thinner consistency. Use nylon brushes for painting, since the chemicals will damage natural bristles.

There are many variables in printing such as the mesh of the screen, the weight of the fabric, and the construction of the fabric, to name a few. These variables often require making changes in a print paste recipe. The above recipe, therefore, is of a general type. Examples of possible variations are:

o More alginate or alginate of a different viscosity might be used in the print paste to hold a slow-drying print in place (fabric with low absorbency or a sheer, lightweight fabric).
o More urea is usually added to the print paste when dry heat is used for fixation.
o When printing black it may be necessary to add less urea and more sodium bicarbonate.

The steps are actually solutions to problems learned through experience and research. A feeling for when these variations are needed will be acquired as you become familiar with the medium.

Fixation of Fiber-Reactive Dye   After printing, most of the dyestuff is still lying on the surface of the fiber. During fixation the dye particles enter and are trapped within the fiber. With fiber-reactives, any unfixed dye will wash away in the after-wash.

There are a number of choices available to the small-scale printer for fixing of fiber-reactive dyes. The methods described here are based on ICI's recommendations for small-scale printing. Before undertaking a fixation process, make sure the fabric is thoroughly dry. Then choose one of the following procedures:

o Steam for 5 to 10 minutes in any available or improvised steam chest. There are several types of steamers that you can easily devise. You can obtain excellent results on small pieces by steaming in a pressure cooker.
o Bake for 5 minutes at 285°F in an oven. More urea might be required with this method to obtain deep colors.
o Iron for 5 minutes with the iron set at 285°F for dry heat, or with steam. This appears to work best on lightweight fabrics. Results may be inconsistent.
o Air dry in a warm, humid atmosphere for 1 to 2 days. If this method is used, it is preferable to replace the $1\frac{1}{2}$ parts sodium bicarbonate in the formula with 1 part sodium bicarbonate and $\frac{1}{2}$ part washing soda. The humidity produced by a bathroom shower often works.
o Before printing, but after washing, soak the cloth for $\frac{1}{2}$ minute in a cold solution of 2 parts sodium carbonate in 100 parts water. Squeeze out the excess solution, dry, and iron. Print, and air dry for 1 to 2 days in a warm, humid atmosphere. If this method is followed, the alkali (sodium bicarbonate) should be omitted from the print paste formula.

After-Wash of Fabrics Printed with Fiber-Reactive Dye

The fabric must be rinsed in constantly running water for 5 minutes to wash away excess dye. The fabric is then washed at as hot a temperature as possible with a home laundry detergent for 5 minutes, and then rinsed.

Screenmaking

The screenmaking procedure is basically the same for paper and textile printing. However, there are a few exceptions.

Silk is generally considered unsuitable for stretching screens used for textile printing. Nylon and polyester are preferred since they are more durable and suitable for direct emulsion screens. Textile printers rely a great deal on direct emulsion screenmaking because of its versatility, relatively low cost, and water-resistant qualities. Furthermore, to remove the image from a direct emulsion screen you would have to use chlorine bleach, which would completely destroy a silk mesh.

Some textile printers use brown paper tape with shellac or lacquer overpainting for taping the edges of the screen, but most prefer waterproof tape (such as white plastic or duct). Waterproof tapes are easier to apply, completely waterproof, and durable. They also eliminate the necessity of overpainting with shellac or lacquer.

Because most textile print pastes are washed from the screen with water, it is especially important to seal a new wood frame with a water-resistant material, such as lacquer or shellac. Otherwise, the frame will warp after some use.

Although direct photo emulsion screens are most common in textile printing, any of the other methods used to produce an image on the screen are suitable, provided the material blocking the screen is not water soluble. Various methods are described in Chapter 4.

Printing Equipment

The Squeegee

The type of squeegee blade used affects the amount of print paste deposited on the fabric. Generally, speaking, rounder, softer squeegees deposit more color, and sharp squeegees deposit less. Although any squeegee will print, for the most effective results a special textile squeegee blade is recommended. These are generally available through screenprinting supply companies. The one-hand squeegee (mentioned for paper printing) generally is not used for textiles.

The Printing Table

For textile printing it is necessary to have a table with a padded and resilient surface. Because fabric is both absorbent and flexible, the table surface must be able to conform to the movement of each particular fabric under the squeegee pressure. The printing table should be level, stable, and a comfortable height (approximately 30 inches high).

Tables can be made from a variety of commonly available materials. The design may be as simple or elaborate as you need. A simple, but adequate printing surface can be constructed easily by the beginner. The top can be made of heavy plywood, or similar material, reinforced and supported underneath by a frame of heavy wood. It is important to have a consistently level, stable surface, and the frame is instrumental in maintaining this. The legs should be made of a sturdy material and attached securely to the frame.

Two layers of $\frac{1}{4}$-inch felt stretched over the table top and tacked or stapled to the sides is a standard table padding. You may choose different padding, but remember to maintain a smooth, preferably seamless surface to avoid print imperfections. The top surface can be made of a number of different materials, such as cloth, vinyl, or rubber. Again, this material must be smooth, not textured. This final layer must be stretched very tightly over the table surface and tacked or stapled to the sides (Fig. 125). A surface that is too loose will buckle when the printer applies pressure to the screen.

Preparation for Printing

When a cloth-top table is used, the fabric to be printed is generally pinned to the surface with T-shape pins (called T pins). These are inserted inward along the edge of the fabric at close and equal intervals. First, pin one long side of the fabric, parallel to the table edge; then pin the opposite edge and the ends, in that order. It is important that the second and last sides are pulled during pinning. This ensures a wrinkle-free, stable fabric. Try to keep the threads of the fabric straight across the table.

Sometimes it is advisable first to pin a *back gray* (backing fabric) to the table before the print cloth. This fabric will absorb excess dye that might go through the print fabric, and will prevent successive prints from picking up color from the table top. This back gray can be washed and reused.

There is usually less need for a back gray on a rubber or vinyl table, because this table can be washed after printing. With a thin or sheer fabric, however, a back gray will provide the absorbency necessary to soak up excess color. Pins are not used on vinyl or rubber tables. Either attach the print fabric with an adhesive directly to the table surface, or pin it to a back gray that has previously been adhered to the table.

The preceding information regarding print tables has been of a general nature. The size of the table and registration systems have not been mentioned. The nature of your own work will determine these specifics. For example, if you want to print repeating images,

125. A table for printing fabrics,
showing cloth or vinyl top surface,
felt padding underneath,
and L-shape rail and stops for registration.

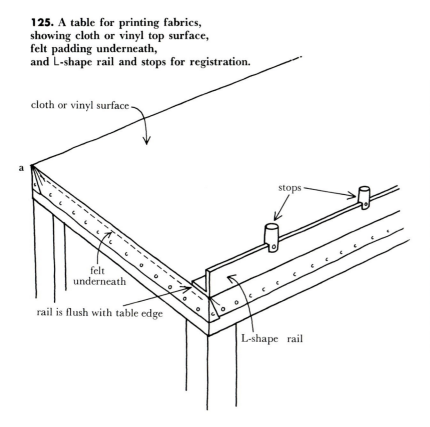

cloth or vinyl surface

a

stops

felt
underneath

rail is flush with table edge

L-shape rail

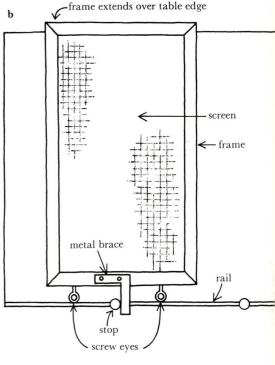

b

frame extends over table edge

screen

frame

metal brace

rail

stop

screw eyes

126. The rail-and-stop registration
system involves an L-shape metal brace
attached to the top of the screen,
with screw eyes inserted on one side
of the frame and against the rail.

you must have a system to guide the placement of the screen. In hand printing on textiles, the fabric is stationary, while the screen is moved. Only a few individual printers reverse this method. A standard device for placement consists of movable stops on an L-shape metal rail attached to one long side of the table (Fig. 125). (When a table has such a rail, the felt should end at the rail, with only the top surface covering extending under the rail, as in Figure 125.) The stops are positioned at the proper intervals along the rail in order to have the printed area repeat accurately as the screen is moved down the table.

This rail-and-stop system can be used when printing images that join inconspicuously, or when printing isolated images with measured spaces between. A rail system generally is not practical or necessary unless the table is at least 3 yards long.

To use the rail system, it is necessary to attach some hardware to the screen. This consists of two screw eyes and an L-shape metal brace. The screw eyes are inserted on one side of the frame. During printing, the screen will be placed on the table with these screw eyes against the rail (Fig. 126). By screwing or unscrewing one or the other of the screw eyes, you can adjust the angle of the screen across the table.

The metal brace is attached to the top surface of the screen with one of its sides extending out over the rail (Fig. 126). This brace rests against the stop when each position is printed.

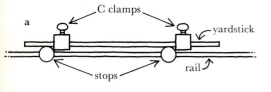

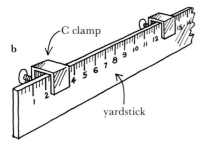

127. Stops for the rail system of registration should be carefully secured by a clamp or gauge bolt (a), at measured intervals along the rail (b).

Printing the Fabric

Printing with Rail Registration

When printing across the full width of a fabric, it will often be necessary to have two people to handle the squeegee. (One person can handle fabrics up to 36 inches wide.)

Stops, such as clamps or gauge bolts, are carefully secured by a screw device at the properly measured intervals along the rail (Fig. 127). The first stop position is determined by placing the screen against the rail where it will print the very beginning of the fabric, and securing the stop next to the brace. This is the first printing position. Measuring must be done from the same side of the stop each time (that is, from right side to right side).

The printers stand on opposite sides of the table and move the squeegee across the screen, passing it smoothly from one person to the other (Fig. 128). It is important that the person opposite the rail lean against the frame of the screen to prevent it from separating from the rail during printing.

Except for very sheer or lightweight fabrics, a textile is seldom printed with one squeegee pass, as in paper printing. Two passes are usual, although thick or rough-surface fabrics may require more.

To continue printing down the fabric length, raise the screen carefully, lifting from one side to the other, and place it at the *third* stop. Alternate positions are printed to avoid resting the screen frame on the previous print, which will still be wet. On a long table the first series of prints will be dry when the printers are ready to return and fill in between. For shorter tables, clean newsprint can be placed over the first prints while the second group is printed. This is not an ideal solution, however, for the wet color may transfer onto the newsprint, leaving an uneven finished print. The safest procedure in this situation is to wash and dry the screen, interrupting the printing until the screen and the first run of prints have dried. Then begin printing the remaining positions.

For some works you may want to print only the edge or a section of the fabric, and perhaps add more to the piece by some other application method, such as hand painting or dyeing. This can be done by pinning the fabric to the table in the usual manner and using a small screen. The printing can be done by one person.

Printing without Registration Systems

When printing on fabric it is not always necessary or desirable to use a system of registration, nor is it always advantageous to have a registration rail on the printing table. Without the rail you can move the screen freely, turning it at whatever angle is necessary (Fig. 129). It is possible to plan the placement of a screen by using masking tape registration marks directly on the fabric. These marks would indicate where the corners of the screen lie.

A single unit can be printed repeatedly to create a more complex visual image. Paper stencils can be taped directly to the fabric for blockout, or portions of an image on a screen can be blocked out with paper, then the remainder printed.

Safety Precautions

The printer working with textile media and chemicals should observe certain precautions. Some dye powders and their respective chemicals can cause skin, eye, and respiratory irritations. Some common-sense rules will help avoid this:

Wear protective clothing such as rubber gloves, aprons, or safety glasses when handling chemicals. Never handle dye powder directly; wear rubber gloves. Avoid inhalation of dye particles by mixing the dye powder into solutions slowly, by working in well-ventilated rooms, and by using a dust mask or respirator. Separate utensils should be used for mixing dye preparations; never borrow utensils meant for food preparation. Avoid working in eating areas, and eating or drinking in work areas. The eyes are susceptible to irritants and should be carefully protected.

Keep the studio clean and dust free. Wipe up any spills, and have simple first aid material available.

left: 128. When using the rail system, two printers on opposite sides of the printing table move the squeegee across the screen. If an especially large frame is involved, a third person may be needed to help secure it.

below: 129. Without a registration system, it is possible to turn the screen to any necessary angle, as shown in this home studio.

NINE

The Curating
of Prints

Paper is a durable yet fragile material. It can last for hundreds of years if it is made carefully with selected materials and cared for properly, but it also can be destroyed easily if made with poor materials or improperly handled, stored, or framed.

Newsprint, made from ground wood pulp, is a paper designed to be short-lived. It becomes brown and brittle within a few years. Other papers of better quality than newsprint often can have extremely limited life spans due to the action of acids or other chemicals left in the fibers; these cause a rapid breakdown in the paper and greatly reduce its longevity. During the period when wood pulp was manufactured on a large scale, particularly from 1900 to about 1940, papermaking methods were employed that left a considerable amount of free acid and other impurities in the paper as a result of chemical reactions between the alum-rosin sizing and moisture in the air. The millions of books and documents printed on this inferior material are now a nightmare to librarians and paper restorers throughout the world. Worse yet is the fact that these inferior papers will contaminate better ones when they are placed in contact with them.

Apart from selecting quality papers whose long life span can be anticipated, the proper care and conservation of paper and valuable works of art on paper is a task that benefits the artist, the museum curator, and the collector alike. Attention must be paid not only to the quality of the paper, but to the way in which it is handled, the conditions and manner in which it is stored, and the other materials with which it comes in contact. With these precautions, prints can remain in excellent condition indefinitely.

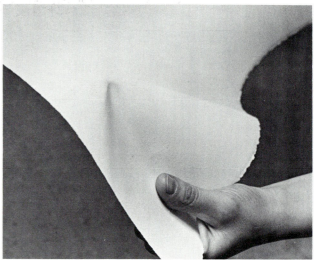

The Care of Prints

Handling Paper

There are special ways to handle paper. Any type of paper can be bruised, creased, wrinkled, or soiled easily. Museum curators and print dealers take many elaborate precautions to prevent improper handling of a print, from placing each work in a plastic envelope to instructing and observing the handler carefully. Yet, in spite of considerable literature on the subject, countless works are wrinkled, creased, stained, discolored, or otherwise mutilated by careless handling or the use of inferior mounting or framing materials.

The following guidelines will help to ensure that proper care is taken of valuable prints.

1. Paper should always be held so that it flows in an even, unbroken wave. It should be grasped carefully between the thumb and fingers at opposite edges or corners in a way that will not cause the paper to buckle (Fig. 130). Faulty handling causes a kink in the paper, and the creases produced are often irreparable (Fig. 131).

2. Prints should be touched only with clean hands or with paper tabs, to protect the edges.

3. Loose prints never should be rolled up for prolonged storage, but should be stored flat in metal or wooden print cabinets, solander boxes, or other flat storage cabinets. Each print should be interleaved with an acid-free tissue, such as tableau tissue, glassine, Japanese mulberry paper, or other inexpensive fine and soft material. Tinted paper, newsprint, or cardboard should not be used for this purpose. If tubes are used for mailing or carrying prints, a large-diameter tube is best, so that the prints will not be rolled tightly. Remove and flatten the prints as soon as possible.

4. Prints should come in contact only with quality rag mounting board with neutral pH or other special papers used for mounting. Cardboard or chipboard, for example, will stain and make the paper brittle in time.
5. Special tapes, such as gummed linen tape (Holland tape) or gummed transparent hinging tape, or adhesives, such as wheat paste or rice starch paste, should be used for mounting.

Trimming Paper

Tearing It is best to maintain the natural deckle of a sheet of paper whenever possible; however, trimming the paper to size is sometimes unavoidable. Most papers can be torn with a heavy metal straightedge or a tearing bar (Fig. 132). The latter device can be constructed from a piece of steel, 18 gauge or thicker, loosely bolted to a table top. For convenience, the front end of the table should have a long ruler or tape permanently affixed to it, though the table itself can be marked for efficient measurement of a given paper size. Place the paper face-down under the tearing bar, because the bar leaves a visible straight line along the deckle on the side of the paper that it contacts. Pull the section to be trimmed up and toward the bar, holding the bar in place with the other hand.

Another way of trimming paper to retain a decklelike edge is to fold it and burnish the fold lightly with a piece of ivory or other smooth tool. Insert a long knife into the fold, and draw the blade slowly against it, making sure that the long blade remains parallel to the paper surface. (It is helpful to work along the end of a table top.)

If a decklelike edge is desired on a quantity of machine-cut or razor-cut paper, the stock should be placed on a workbench, overlapping the end of the bench top by about ¼ inch. A piece of wood 1 by 3 inches and longer than the edge being trimmed should be placed on the top of the stack ¼ inch back from the edge, and held in place by another person or clamped in place with moderate pressure. A wood rasp is then drawn against the end of the stack of paper, creating a consistent rough edge on each individual sheet. If a natural deckle is to be feigned on only a few sheets, place the paper face-down and scrape the edge with a razor. Working at a slight angle will feather the paper toward the edge and create the most natural-looking deckle, although it is a tedious job.

Razor Cutting If a single edge is to be razor cut, the tearing bar or a straightedge will do. A board at least ⅛ inch thick should be placed on the table top to protect it. When all four edges must be razor cut, as is more often the case, it is most efficient to make a template, preferably of metal, to the desired format. Formica, Masonite, or Plexiglas will also serve the purpose, but greater care must be taken to avoid cutting into the template.

132. Tearing paper with a metal straightedge.

Matting the Print

Because the damage done to a framed print is concealed, it often goes unnoticed for years. Cheap varieties of cardboard, chipboard, corrugated board, and other backing materials can be extremely harmful to the print when placed in direct contact with it, and should be used for temporary support only. These wood pulp cardboards contain noticeable amounts of acid, which stain the fibers of the print in time. The acidic content also weakens the cellulose fibers in the paper, changing their color and causing them to become brittle.

The best mat boards are the all-rag mounting boards (often called museum mounting boards), available in several different weights and sizes. They are usually a white or yellowish buff color and display the same color throughout when cut. For large prints, the heavier weight rag mat board will be necessary. Hot-pressed, heavyweight watercolor paper also will make an excellent substitute matting or backing material. Cheaper mat boards have wood pulp centers and surfaces of better grade paper. Although these are commonly used for much of the framing done in the United States and are available in a wide range of tones and colors, museums and institutions always avoid them because of their tendency to discolor paper. Some recommended types of museum mounting boards include W & A (Cream), Gemini (White), Lenox (Bright White), and Bainbridge All-Rag Museum Mounting Board (White or Ivory). All come in 2-ply and 4-ply weights, in sheets measuring 22 by 32 inches, 32 by 40 inches, and 40 by 60 inches. An excellent barrier paper that can be put between the print and the backing board if necessary is A/N/W Drawing-Framing Paper. This is a single-ply (cream) stock, available in rolls 60 inches by 29 yards.

Cutting the mat requires skill. The equipment needed includes a sturdy table, a heavyweight metal straightedge, a mat knife or utility knife, and a compass. Learn to sharpen the blade of the knife and keep the cutting edge well honed during the cutting. This will improve the results and make the job easier. Cutting through the board should be done with a single stroke if possible, to produce the cleanest edge. For a straight cut on extra heavy board, hold the metal straightedge firmly against a lightly penciled line, and cut the board with a light stroke, then with a heavier one to cut through completely. Thin boards should be cut in a single stroke (Fig. 133).

The beveled mat is a little more difficult to cut. Some mat cutters prefer to cut from the back of the mat, others from the face. Both methods are good, although there are advantages to cutting from the back. Pencil lines made on the back to indicate the mat opening can be erased afterwards, and the corners do not show the slight overcutting made by the knife.

To cut a beveled mat from the back, measure the size of the opening and subtract this from the width of the mat. Divide the

133. Thin mat board can be cut with a single stroke of the knife.

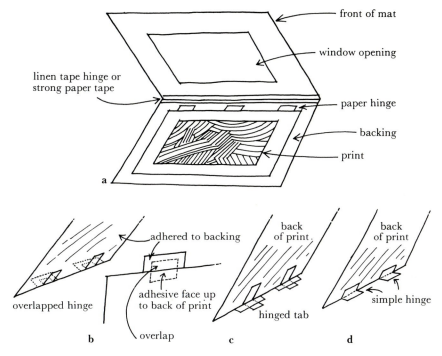

front of mat

window opening

linen tape hinge or
strong paper tape

paper hinge

backing

print

a

adhered to backing

adhesive face up
to back of print

back
of print

back
of print

overlapped hinge

overlap

hinged tab

simple hinge

b   c   d

134. The basic mat (a).
Hinges to attach the print
to the backing include
the overlapped hinge (b),
the hinged tab (c),
and the simple hinge (d).

remainder in half to find the margin width, and—with this measurement set on the compass—run the metal point of the compass
along the outside edges of the mat, making parallel pencil lines on
opposite sides. The margins on the top and sides are usually equal,
with the bottom slightly wider, although the proportions will depend on the size and character of the individual print. Normal
margin widths are between 2 and 6 inches.

The ordinary mat knife can become the simplest and most
practical device for cutting mats, after a little practice. Mat-cutting
units, like the Keeton Kutter made by Bainbridge, facilitate the
cutting procedure. They can cut straight or beveled edges and lessen
the need for pencil lines on the mat.

Two boards of equal size are used for each mat—one for the
backing board and one for the open window. The front window mat
is hinged to the backing board along the top or on the left side,
whichever is longer (Fig. 134). Use either a special linen tape with a
water-soluble, nonstaining, nonacidic adhesive, or a strip of mulberry or other strong Oriental paper with wheat or rice paste.

The print can then be positioned under the opening and hinged
at the top with additional strips of linen tape or Oriental paper,
such as *hosho,* mulberry, or *kozo* paper. Scotch tape, masking tape,
rubber cement, gummed tape, and heat-sealing tissues should be
avoided. They discolor the paper, often irreparably, and most lose
their adhesive quality within a year or so. Hinges can be made in
various ways, as shown in Figure 134. If a buildup in the combined
thicknesses of the layers of tape becomes a problem, method **a**

135. The traditional framing arrangement (a):
a recommended framing method
for use with aluminum section frames
to produce a moisture-proof unit (b),
and a method of framing a floated print (c).

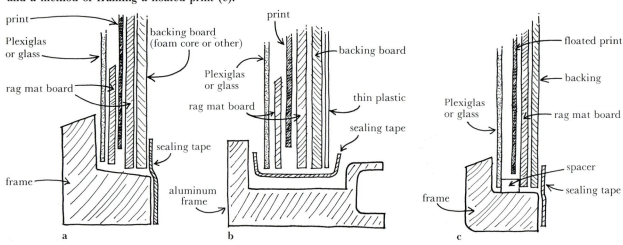

should be used. Once the hinge has been attached, the print and backing board are placed under a heavy weight to ensure flatness. A sheet of blotter paper should be placed between the weight and the print for protection.

Making a French mat is an expensive procedure aesthetically suited to a more decorative approach to matting and framing. It consists of accurately ruled lines of differing widths on the face of the mat, forming a decorative color border along the edge of the opening. The area between two lines is often filled with a subtle watercolor wash in a tone coordinated with the colors of the print.

Framing the Print

The selection of a frame is an aesthetic and economic consideration ultimately dependent upon the object to be framed. Three basic ways of framing are shown in Figure 135. Method **b** is ideal for making the print impervious to moisture, because the matted unit is sandwiched between Plexiglas on the front and Mylar or acetate on the back and sealed with strong plastic or cloth tape on the edges.

Metal frames can be purchased readymade or in sections that can be put together at home. They are excellent for framing contemporary prints, and are best used in conjunction with Plexiglas, because this eliminates the danger of breakage. Always a problem with a glass-covered frame, breakage is particularly likely in metal frames in which the metal contacts the glass directly.

The print never should be placed in direct contact with glass or Plexiglas. If the print is very large, making matting difficult, a small spacer or fillet should be used. If contact is unavoidable, use Plexiglas instead of glass. Because glass reacts to atmospheric conditions, it allows moisture to condense on the inside, and this moisture will almost certainly stain the print.

List of Suppliers

Many materials such as solvents, brushes, paper, and tools can be obtained from a well-stocked hardware or art supply store. Consult the yellow pages for local commercial printing, chemical, and plastics suppliers.

General Supplies

Arthur Brown and Bro., Inc., 2 West 46th Street, New York, N.Y. 10036

David Davis (Fine Arts Materials Company), 539 La Guardia Place, New York, N.Y. 10012

M. Flax, 10852 Lindbrook Drive, Los Angeles, Calif. 90024

Sam Flax, 25 East 28th Street, New York, N.Y. 10016

Graphic Chemical and Ink Co., P.O. Box 27, Villa Park, Ill. 60181

New York Central Supply Co., 82 Third Avenue, New York, N.Y. 10003

Rembrandt Graphic Arts Co., The Cane Farm, Rosemont N.J. 08556

Screenprinting General Supplies

Active Process Supply Co., Inc., 15 W. 20th Street, New York, N.Y. 10011

Advance Process Supply Co., 6900 River Road, Pennsauken, N.J. 08110; 400 West Noble Street, Chicago, Ill. 60622; 3101 San Jacinto, Houston, Texas 77004; 570 McDonald Avenue, Brooklyn, N.Y. 11218; and 268 Eddystone Road, Downsview, Toronto, Ontario, Canada

Dick Blick, P.O. Box 1267, Galesburg, Ill. 61401

Bona Venture Supply Co., 17 Village Square, St. Louis, Missouri 63042

Colonial Printing Ink Co., 180 East Union Avenue, East Rutherford, N.J. 07073

Naz-Dar Co., 33 Lafayette Avenue, Brooklyn, N.Y. 11217; 1087 North Branch Street, Chicago, Ill. 60622; 12800 Woodrow Wilson, Detroit, Michigan 48238; 2832 South Alameda, Los Angeles, Calif. 90058; and 925 Roselawn Avenue, Toronto 19, Ontario, Canada

Standard Screen Supply Co., 15 West 20th Street, New York, N.Y. 10011

Dyes

Ciba Chemical and Dye Co. (for prompt service direct all inquiries to nearest district sales office), 1815 South Hamilton Park, Whitfield Industrial Park, Dalton, Georgia 30720; Route 208, Fairlawn, N.J. 07410; Suite 305, 6279 East Slauson Avenue, Los Angeles, Calif. 90022; 4241 North Second Street, Philadelphia, Penn. 19140; 331 North Broadway, Rumford, R.I. 02900; and 7355 Lincoln Avenue, Skokie, Ill. 60076

FAB/DEC, 540 West Armitage, Chicago, Ill. 60614

I.C.I. America, Inc., Box 1274, 151 South Street, Stamford, Conn. 06904

Keystone Aniline and Chemical Co., Inc., 321 North Loomis Street, Chicago, Ill. 60607

Dyestuffs for Textile Printing

Batik International, P.O. Box 659, Del Mar, Calif. 92014

Cerulean Blue Ltd., P.O. Box 5126, 1314 N.E. 43rd Street, Seattle, Wash. 98105

Dharma Trading Co., P.O. Box 1288T, 1952 University Avenue, Berkeley, Calif. 94701

D.Y.E., 3763 Durango Avenue, Los Angeles, Calif. 90034

FAB/DEC, 3553 Old Post Road, San Angelo, Texas 76901

Pro-Chemical and Dye Co., P.O. Box 1192, Fairfield, Conn. 06432

Pylan, 95-10 218th Street, Queens Village, N.Y. 11429

Screen Process Supplies Manufacturing Co., 1199 East 12th Street, Oakland, Calif. 94606

Wildflowers Fibers, 211 N.W. Davis Street, Portland, Oregon 97200

Lacquer Film

Ulano Products Co., Inc., 210 East 86th Street, New York, N.Y. 10028

Lacquer Film Cutters

The Ramsey Co., 2701 South Ervay Street, Dallas, Texas 75215

Ulano Products Co., Inc., 210 East 86th Street, New York, N.Y. 10028

Metal Powders

Alcan Metal Powders, P.O. Box 290, Elizabeth, N.J. 07207

Photo Gelatin and Carbon Tissue

McGraw Film Co., 175 West Verdugo Avenue, Burbank, Calif. 91503

Norfilm Corp. (Autotype U.S.A.), P.O. Box 267, Parkchester Station, Bronx, New York 10462

Pigments

Fezandie and Sperrle, Inc., 111 Eighth Avenue, New York, N.Y. 10011

Inmont Corp., Printing Ink Division, St. Mark Street, Auburn, Mass. 01501

Pigment Print Paste (Textile Printing)

Active Process Supply Co., Inc. (Fab-Tone), 15 West 20th Street, New York, N.Y. 10011

Advance Process Supply Co. (Aqua-Set), 6900 River Road, Pennsauken, N.J. 08110; 400 West Noble Street, Chicago, Ill. 60622; 3101 San Jacinto, Houston, Texas 77004; 570 McDonald Avenue, Brooklyn, N.Y. 11218; and 268 Eddystone Road, Downsview, Toronto, Canada

Bona Venture Supply Co. (Versatex), 17 Village Square, St. Louis, Missouri 63042

Pearl Paint Co., Inc. (Versatex), 308 Canal Street, New York, N.Y. 10011

Sax Arts and Crafts (Colortex), P.O. Box 2002, Milwaukee, Wis. 53201

Vacuum Forming

AAA Plastic Equipment, 2617 North Ayers, Fort Worth, Texas 76103

Plasti-Vac, Inc., 214 Dalton Avenue, Charlotte, N.C. 28205

Vacuum Frames and Reproduction Cameras

Nu Arc Co., Ltd., 175 Varick Street, New York, N.Y. 10014

Paper

Andrews/Nelson/Whitehead, 31-10 48th Avenue, Long Island City, N.Y. 11101

Laurence Barker, Ganduxer, 5, 1-7, B, Barcelona 6, Spain

Dick Blick, P.O. Box 1267, Galesburg, Ill. 61401

Crestwood Paper Corp., 263 Ninth Avenue, New York, N.Y. 10001

David Davis (Find Arts Materials Company), 539 La Guardia Place, New York, N.Y. 10012

Farnsworth and Serpa Handmade Paper Mill, 1333 Wood Street, Oakland, Calif. 94607

HMP Papers, Barlow Cemetery Road, Woodstock Valley, Conn. 06282

Guy T. Kuhn, Box 166, Keedysville, Md. 21756

New York Central Supply Co., 82 Third Avenue, New York, N.Y. 10003

Rembrandt Graphic Arts Co., The Cane Farm, Rosemont, N.J. 08556

Special Papers, Inc. West Redding, Conn. 06896

Twinrocker Handmade Paper, Brookston, Indiana 47923

Upper U.S. Papermill, 999 Glenway Road, Oregon, Wis. 53575

Matting Board

Andrews/Nelson/Whitehead, 31-10 48th Avenue, Long Island City, N.Y. 11101

Charles T. Bainbridge's Sons, 20 Cumberland Street, Brooklyn, N.Y. 11205

Zellerbach Paper Co., 4000 East Union Pacific Avenue, Los Angeles, Calif. 90054

Transparent Hinging Tape

Talas, 104 Fifth Avenue, New York, N.Y. 10011

Acid-Free Storage Folder

Hollinger Corp., P.O. Box 6185, Arlington, Va. 22206

Spink and Gaborc, Inc. (portfolios and solander boxes), 32 West 18th Street, New York, N.Y. 10003

Talas (solander boxes), 104 Fifth Avenue, New York, N.Y. 10011

Screen Presses

Advance Process Supply Co., 6900 River Road, Pennsauken, N.J. 08110; 400 West Noble Street, Chicago, Ill. 60622; 3101 San Jacinto, Houston, Texas 77004; 570 McDonald Avenue, Brooklyn, N.Y. 11218; and 268 Eddystone Road, Downsview, Toronto, Ontario, Canada

Colonial Printing Ink Co., 180 East Union Avenue, East Rutherford, N.J. 07073

Naz-Dar Co., 33 Lafayette Avenue, Brooklyn, N.Y. 11217; 1087 North Branch Street, Chicago, Ill. 60622; 12800 Woodrow Wilson, Detroit, Michigan 48238; 2832 South Alameda, Los Angeles, Calif. 90058; and 925 Roselawn Avenue, Toronto 19, Ontario, Canada

Bibliography

General Works:

Brunner, Felix. *A Handbook of Graphic Reproduction Processes.* New York: Hastings House Publishers, Inc., 1962.

Eichenberg, Fritz. *The Art of the Print.* New York: Abrams, 1976.

Heller, Jules. *Printmaking Today.* New York: Holt, Rinehart & Winston, 1972.

Hollander, Harry B. *Plastics: For Artists and Craftsmen.* New York: Watson-Guptill, 1972.

Mayer, Ralph. *The Artist's Handbook of Materials and Techniques.* 3rd revised ed. New York: Viking Press, 1970.

Newman, Thelma R. *Plastics as an Art Form.* Philadelphia and New York: Chilton, 1969.

Ross, John, and Clare Romano. *The Complete Printmaker.* New York: The Free Press, 1972.

Technique:

American Fabrics Magazine, editors of. *Encyclopedia of Textiles.* Englewood Cliffs, N.J.: Prentice-Hall, 1960.

Auvil, Kenneth W. *Serigraphy: Silk Screen Techniques for the Artist.* Englewood Cliffs, N.J.: Prentice-Hall, 1965.

Biegeleisen, J. I. *Screen Printing: A Contemporary Guide.* New York: Watson-Guptill, 1971.

Carr, Francis. *A Guide to Screen Process Printing.* London: Vista, 1961.

Chieffo, Clifford T. *Silk Screen as a Fine Art: A Handbook of Contemporary Silk Screen Printing.* New York: Van Nostrand Reinhold Co., 1967.

Cronar Screen Process Film, E. I. Dupont De Nemours & Co., Photo Products Department, Wilmington, Delaware.

Fossett, Robert O. *Techniques in Photography for the Silk Screen Printer.* Cincinnati: Signs of the Times, 1959.

Gardner, Andrew B. *The Artist's Silkscreen Manual.* New York: Grosset and Dunlap, 1976.

Kinsey, Anthony. *Introducing Screen Printing.* New York: Watson-Guptill, 1968.

Kosloff, Albert. *Ceramic Screen Printing.* Cincinnati: Signs of the Times, 1962.

———. *Photographic Screen Printing.* Cincinnati: Signs of the Times, 1972.

———. *Screen Printing Techniques.* Cincinnati: Signs of the Times, 1976.

Marsh, Roger. *Silk Screen Printing.* New York: St. Martin's Press, Inc., 1974.

Reinke, William A. *Silk Screen Printing.* Oil Color Litho Company.

Roberts, Edith A. "Silk Screen Printing with Anthrasol Indigosol Dyes." *Craft Horizons,* Vol. 18, p. 40, September/October 1958.

Russ, Stephen. *Practical Screen Printing.* New York: Watson-Guptill, 1969.

Schwalback, M. V., and J. A. Schwalback. *Screen Process Printing.* New York: Van Nostrand Reinhold Co., 1970.

Steffen, Bernard. *Silk Screen.* London: Pitman, 1963.

Sternberg, Harry. *Silk Screen Color Printing.* New York: McGraw-Hill, 1942.

Textile Printing:

Johnston, Meda P., and Glen Kaufman. *Design on Fabrics.* New York: Van Nostrand Reinhold, 1976.

Kosloff, Albert. *Textile Screen Printing.* Cincinnati: Signs of the Times, 1966.

Lauterberg, Lotti. *Fabric Printing.* New York: Van Nostrand Reinhold, 1962.

Proctor, Richard M. *The Principles of Pattern.* New York: Van Nostrand Reinhold, 1972.

Proud, Nora. *Textile Printing and Dyeing Simplified.* New York: Arco Publishing Co., Inc., 1974.

Robinson, Stuart. *A History of Printed Textiles.* Cambridge, Mass.: M.I.T. Press, 1970.

Robinson, Stuart, and Patricia Robinson. *Exploring Fabric Printing.* Newton Center, Mass.: Charles T. Branford Co., 1972.

Russ, Stephen. *Fabric Printing by Hand.* New York: Watson-Guptill, 1965.

Searle, Valerie, and Roberta Clayson. *Screen Printing on Fabric.* New York: Watson-Guptill, 1968.

Glossary

acetate A clear plastic material obtainable in a variety of weights, sometimes with a frosted finish. It is useful for handmade *positives* in making photo *stencils.*

acetic acid (CH₃COOH) A mild acid used for cleaning *screens,* among other applications.

acetone A highly volatile aromatic hydrocarbon, used as a solvent for hardened *ink* and lacquer; one of the main ingredients in *lacquer thinners.*

adhering fluid A specially prepared solution for adhering hand-cut *stencils* to the *screen.* For *lacquer stencils,* a special *lacquer thinner;* for water-adhering hand-cut films, water and alcohol or alcohol and dilute *acetic acid.*

airbrush An image-making technique in which *tusche* is blown onto a *screen* instead of being brushed or penned on.

alcohol A volatile hydrocarbon used—in ethyl, methyl, or isopropyl forms—as a shellac solvent.

alpha pulp A wood *pulp* composed of pure cellulose fibers.

aluminum stearate A fine powder mixed with a *vehicle* and used as a transparent *extender* and thickening agent.

ammonium bichromate A bright orange crystalline powder used, in water solution, to sensitize *screen* photo *emulsions.*

animal sized A term referring to paper *sized* with a *gelatin* solution.

artist's proof One of a small group of *prints* set aside from the *edition* for the artist's use. Also called *épreuve d'artiste.*

back gray A fabric such as cotton muslin put on a table before textile printing to absorb excess dye from the print fabric.

backprinting A situation in which the image is offset on the underside of the *screen* when printing on fabrics.

benzene A volatile solvent containing benzol, having extremely toxic vapors. This should not be confused with benzine (*naphtha*).

binder A substance that holds together the particles of *pigment* in an *ink* or paint.

binding varnish A clear varnish used as a printing adhesive for *flocking* materials. Added in small amounts to an *ink,* it increases flexibility and scuff resistance.

bleach A solution that removes color or stain. Either the hypochlorite or the chlorine form will remove direct screen *emulsions* after printing and remove stains from *screen* fabric. Bleach cannot be used with silk.

bled print A *print* in which the image extends to one or more edges of the paper.

bleeding *Ink* seepage around a printed image, caused by excessive use of ink, oil, or pressure.

blinding The inability of an image area to accept *ink.*

blockout A substance, either brushed or *squeegeed* onto the *screen* fabric, that prevents *ink* from passing through.

bloom Special color quality apparent in fabrics which have been screenprinted; not present in fabrics printed by other methods.

bon à tirer proof The "right to print" *proof,* designated by the artist as the standard against which every *print* in the *edition* is to be judged for its aesthetic and technical merits.

bridge A band to prevent floating parts of a solid stencil from falling off the *screen.*

broadside Originally, sheets of paper containing printed satire or commentary on one side only. Now refers to any large printed and folded sheet.

bronzing Dusting metallic powder onto a freshly printed image. Metallic *inks* now available may replace this technique.

brush printing Printing through *stencils* onto fabric with stiff brushes applied manually. The process was used mainly before World War I and was later replaced with pressurized spray techniques.

calender System of large horizontal rollers for smoothing out the surface of a finished sheet of paper.

carbon tetrachloride An extremely poisonous solvent that has fallen into disuse and is difficult to obtain.

carbon tissue *Gelatin*-coated paper that can be made *light-sensitive.*

casein glue A white glue that dries colorless. When thinned with water, it is used to adhere textiles temporarily to a surface during printing.

catalytic inks *Inks,* such as "epoxy" inks, made in two parts, one a catalyst that brings about a chemical change in the molecular structure to effect a *cure.*

caustic soda (sodium hydroxide) A strong degreasing solution, sometimes called *lye.* Mixed with water, it cleans *nylon* or *polyester* screens.

chalking In printing, the flaking or rubbing off of dry *pigment,* caused by insufficient *binder* in the *ink.*

chop Identifying mark impressed on a *print* by the printer or workshop, or in some cases by the artist or a collector. Also called *dry stamp.*

circle cutter A compass-like device used for cutting circles in hand-cut *stencils.*

clear base A transparent *extender* for *inks* that increases flexibility and scuff resistance.

cold-press finish A rough or smooth texture made on a sheet of paper by running it through a series of cooled metal cylinders. Compare *hot-press finish.*

color separation The process of making a separate *screen* for each color to be printed.

composite print A *print* that combines other graphic techniques—such as lithography—with the screenprint.

conté Greaseless brown, red, or black semihard chalk or crayon with a fine texture.

continuous-tone image A photographic image—either positive or negative—that contains a full gradation of tonalities.

copy camera See *process camera.*

crock To rub off. Applies to textile printing when pigment print paste is printed on shiny or slick fabrics.

cure To change the physical properties of a substance by means of a chemical reaction, usually with heat. Also called *set.*

dacron (polyester) A strong multifilament or monofilament fiber used to make *screen* fabric.

dark reaction Hardening of film or *light-sensitive screens* that are stored in the dark for a long period of time.

decal (decalcomania) A transfer process in which an image is first printed onto a temporary support covered with a water-soluble coating. When wet with water, the printed area can be lifted and transferred to another surface. Used frequently in transferring images to ceramic ware.

dimensional stability The tendency of a material, such as a sheet of paper, not to shrink or stretch under pressure or other stress.

direct emulsion Technique of making photo screens using a *light-sensitive* solution that is applied to the *screen* before exposure.

discharge printing A process in which fabric is first dyed and then printed with a paste containing bleach.

documentation sheet Form identifying the technique employed in making a *print,* as well as the *inks,* paper, drawing materials, and the size of the *edition.*

double film-line cutter A *stencil*-cutting tool consisting of twin blades, often adjustable, for cutting lines of even width.

dry stamp See *chop.*

duotone *Halftone* image printed first in a color, then in black.

durometer An instrument that measures hardness in rubber materials. For *squeegee* blades, a 45 durometer reading is considered soft, an 80 hard.

dye paste A viscous solution containing dyes and other ingredients to be screened onto fabric.

edition Set of identical *prints,* sometimes numbered and signed, that have been *pulled* by or under the supervision of the artist and are authorized for distribution.

emulsion A homogenous mixture of two normally incompatible substances, such as oil and water.

enamel inks Special *inks* that dry to a hard, generally glossy surface. Some enamels need to be baked in a kiln for permanent applications.

enzyme cleaner A substance containing enzymes that, when mixed with water, is applied to *gelatin* bond films after printing. The enzymes digest the gelatin protein and assist in the cleaning operation.

épreuve d'artiste French term for *artist's proof.*

épreuve d'état French term for *state proof.*

evaporation inks *Inks,* such as poster inks, that dry by solvent evaporation.

extender An inexpensive clear substance added to an *ink* in order to increase its coverage.

fiber-reactive dye a colorfact dye developed in the 1950s that makes a permanent, direct chemical bond with fiber.

fixation In textile printing, the attachment of colorants to a fabric by the application of heat.

flash point The temperature at which a liquid will ignite in the air.

flocked print A *screenprint* made with an adhesive varnish over which wool or rayon flakes have been sprinkled.

flood stroke A technique for filling the *screen* with *ink* before each *print* to prevent it from drying out. The *squeegee* distributes ink across the screen in the opposite direction from that of the printing stroke.

fluorescent ink A luminescent *ink* that absorbs and transmits light either in the dark (phosphorescent) or by increased reflectance due to the existing light sources.

foxing Brown stains produced by the chemical reaction of bacteria on the iron salts in a sheet of paper.

gelatin A water-soluble protein that can be made *light-sensitive;* commonly used for making indirect photo *stencils.*

glacial acetic acid Concentrated pure *acetic acid* (CH_3COOH).

glycerin A drying retarder for printing with water-base tempera.

halftone A photographic image that has been broken up into dots of varying sizes to achieve the effect of a full range of tonalities.

halftone screen A grid of opaque lines that breaks up tonalities on a photographic image into dots of varying sizes.

halo An oil ring sometimes left around an image printed with an oil-base ink.

hand The tactile characteristics of a fabric after it has been screenprinted.

hard sizing A method of *sizing* paper in which the paper is dipped into the size solution, dried, and dipped again. Compare *soft sizing.*

hickey On a *print,* an unwanted spot of *ink* with a white ring around it, caused by dirt in the ink.

hide glue A heavy brown water-soluble glue used as a *blockout* in various screen techniques.

hot-press finish A smooth, often glazed surface, produced on a sheet of paper by running it through a series of heated metal cylinders. Compare *cold-press finish.*

hydrogen peroxide A chemical used as a developer in some indirect photo-*stencil* methods.

impasto On a *print,* a raised area produced by a very heavy layer of *ink.*

impression See *print.*

impression number The number of a *print* in an *edition.* The first three prints in an edition of one hundred would be numbered 1/100, 2/100, 3/100.

indirect photo stencil A photoscreen process in which the stencil is prepared, exposed, and developed before adhesion to the *screen.*

ink Coloring matter composed of *pigment,* a *binder,* and a *vehicle.*

island A floating part of a paper *stencil* that will fall away if not attached by a *bridge.*

kerosene A solvent and thinner for ethyl cellulose *inks;* also retards drying time.

lacquer inks Brilliant and durable *inks* suitable for *decals* and for exterior surfaces of such objects as ceramic ware.

lacquer stencil In hand *stencil* cutting, a lacquer film adhered first to a temporary support and then to the *screen* with *lacquer thinner*.

lacquer thinner Strong solvent for lacquers and other *inks*.

latex Liquid rubber solution used as a marking substance in liquid *blockout*.

length Description of the consistency of an *ink*. A long ink is elastic and rubbery. Compare *shortness*.

lightfastness The ability of a dyed paper or an *ink* to resist changing color when exposed to light.

light-sensitivity The ability of a substance or surface to change chemically when exposed to light.

line shot Black-and-white photographic *negative* or *positive* made on high-contrast film without a *halftone screen* and used for black-and-white copy only or for special effects.

lithotine Substitute for *turpentine*.

livering Thickening of ink caused by oxidation of the oil *vehicle*.

lye See *caustic soda*.

mask stencil A *stencil* in which *ink* is applied to the background, around the outer margins of the image.

mesh size Means of measuring the fineness of a fabric, usually expressed as a number followed by one or more X's.

mezzotint screen Tonal screen for *halftone* photography, employing a random pattern of dots.

mineral spirits Thinner for paints, *tusche*, and all varnish- or oil-base *inks*. Commonly called *paint thinner*.

mitography Synonym for *screenprinting* proposed by Albert Kosloff but never widely adopted.

moiré pattern Optical effect caused by the misalignment of two strongly patterned surfaces so that a third distinctive pattern is formed.

monofilament fiber A fiber consisting of a single continuous filament; by extension, a *screen* mesh in which each thread of both warp and woof consist of a single filament.

multifilament fiber A fiber composed of two or more individual strands; by extension, a *screen* mesh in which each fiber consists of two or more filaments.

naphtha (benzine) A highly volatile, flammable solvent sometimes used for diluting oil-base *inks* and cleaning them from *screens*.

negative Photographic image in which the areas of light and shade are the reverse of their appearance in the original. Compare *positive*.

negative stencil A *stencil* on which the background is the actual printing area. Compare *positive stencil*.

nylon A strong *screen* fabric material made only in *monofilament*.

opacity coverage The area that can be covered by a given amount of *ink*. This is expressed in gallons per square foot.

oxidation inks Printing *inks* that harden chemically as they are exposed to the air and, when dry, become insoluble in their original solvent.

paint thinner See *mineral spirits*.

pH scale In chemistry, a scale of values from 0 to 14, measuring the acidity or alkalinity of a substance. A pH value of 7 is neutral. Numbers less than 7 indicate more acidity; those greater than 7 indicate more alkalinity.

photo opaque A substance, often black or red, that is painted onto film *negatives* and *positives* to prevent the passage of light.

photosilkscreen Technique for the transfer of photographic images to a *stencil* for *screenprinting*.

pigment Coloring matter in *ink* or paint, usually in powder form.

pochoir Printmaking technique using a *stencil* made of plastic, brass, copper, or oiled paper, through which color is dabbed, brushed, or rolled onto the print surface.

polyester Fabric of excellent dimensional stability and strength used for making *screens*. Available in either multifilament or monofilament weave.

positive Photographic image in which the areas of light and shade correspond to the original image. Compare *negative*.

positive stencil *Stencil* in which the image is the printing area. Compare *negative stencil*.

posterization A photographic technique for producing sharp and dramatic images by making variable exposures of a *continuous-tone image*.

potassium bichromate A *light-sensitive* salt used, mixed with water, as a sensitizer for direct-screen *emulsions;* not as light-sensitive as *ammonium bichromate*.

presensitized film Photo *stencil* film material already sensitized and ready for exposure.

presentation proofs *Prints* outside the *edition,* generally intended as gifts.

print Image produced on paper or another material by placing it in contact with an inked block, plate, collage, or stone and applying pressure; or by pressing *ink* onto a sheet of paper through a *stencil*. Also called an *impression*.

printer's proofs *Prints* outside the *edition,* given to the master printer and the printer-collaborator, if any.

process camera Large camera unit used for photo-printmaking techniques. Also called a *copy camera*.

progressive proofs Series of *proofs* for a multicolor *print,* showing each of the colors individually and with the other colors.

proof Trial *print pulled* to test the progress of the image.

pull To *print* an image.

pulp The basic ingredient of paper, consisting of cotton or vegetable fibers that have been chopped and beaten in water so that the fibers are properly fibrillated.

pumice A fine abrasive powder made from volcanic ash used in cleaning and preparing *screens*.

quire Twenty-four sheets of paper.

rag paper Fine paper for printing, made from 100 percent cotton or linen fibers and not containing any wood *pulp*.

ream Five hundred sheets of paper. For wrapping tissues, a ream is 480 sheets.

register marks Marks drawn to aid in *registration*. They are usually in the form of a small cross or triangle.

registration Adjustment of separate *screens* in color printing to ensure correct alignment of the colors.

resist See *blockout*.

retarder Liquid used to slow drying time and prevent clogging of the *screen*.

scooper coater Metal trough used for applying direct photo *emulsions* to the *screen*.

scooper cutter Tool with special cutting edge, in the form of a small circle of steel, which is used for making lines in lacquer stencil films or water-soluble hand-cut films.

screen A fabric mesh of silk, nylon, or polyester that contains the image for the screenprint and through which *ink* or dye is forced by the *squeegee*.

screenprinting Printing technique that makes use of a *squeegee* to force *ink* or dye directly onto paper, fabric, or other material through a *stencil* containing the image. The process is also called *silkscreen, serigraphy,* or (seldom) *mitography.*

serigraphy Alternate term for *screenprinting.*

set See *cure.*

set-off Impression made on the back of a sheet of paper by a wet print underneath it.

shortness Description of the consistency of an *ink*. A short ink is buttery and stiff, breaking away from the printing surface easily and without forming strings. Compare *length*.

silkscreen See *screenprinting.*

sizing *Gelatinous* substance that reduces the absorbency of a sheet of paper. Compare *hard sizing; soft sizing.*

slipsheet A sheet of tissue or newsprint placed over a wet *print* to prevent *set-off* of wet *ink* onto other prints placed on top.

soft sizing Method of *sizing* paper by dipping it into the size solution once. Compare *hard sizing.*

solander box Flat box for storing *prints*. It opens up for display purposes.

squeegee A tool for pushing *ink* through the *screen*. It consists of a handle and a wooden or metal casing holding a hard rubber or plastic blade.

state proof Series of *proofs* taken after each of the steps in the completion of a *print*. Also called *épreuve d'état.*

stencil A means of blocking the passage of *ink* through the nonimage areas of the *screen*. A *stencil* can be made of paper, glue, *tusche*, shellac, or a variety of other materials.

struck off *Printed, pulled.*

suite Related group of original *prints*.

tack Stickiness of an *ink*.

thermosetting inks *Inks* that must be heated after printing in order to dry them.

thixotropy The property of an *ink* that renders it more flexible when worked and less flexible after standing.

thread count Number of threads per inch in a fabric, as a *screen* fabric.

tooth The roughness of the *screen* fabric, produced by means of special abrasives.

transparent base Heavy viscous substance composed of *aluminum stearate, mineral spirits,* and other ingredients and used both to extend *inks* and make them transparent.

trap The slight overlapping of two areas of color on a *print*. Also the ability of a color to adhere to another color (known as trapping).

trial proof Initial *proof pulled* to check the appearance of the image.

trisodium phosphate A strong degreasing agent used to prepare *screens* for use.

turpentine Solvent used to clean *screens* after printing. Excellent for use with ethyl cellulose *inks*.

tusche Grease-based drawing material used for some types of *stencils*. It contains wax, tallow, soap, shellac, and lampblack, and comes in solid and liquid form.

vehicle Liquid ingredient of an *ink* or paint that allows the *pigment* to be applied easily to a surface.

vellum Early type of paper made from the skin of sheep, goats, or hogs. Also called parchment. Many commercial vellums are high rag content papers of different weights, often semi-transparent.

viscosity In an *ink* or dye, the resistance of the liquid to flow or movement.

water-base textile ink *Ink* compounded of dye and a water-base *vehicle* for use on textiles; requires heat setting after printing.

water-in-ink emulsion Fine water droplets surrounded by oil-base *ink*.

waterleaf paper Paper without *sizing*.

watermark Image made within a sheet of paper by variations in *pulp* thickness.

xylol A solvent and thinner for ethyl cellulose *inks* or rubber cement. Used also as a strong solvent for dried *ink*.

Index

Photographic Sources

Oscar Bailey (119, 121); Rudolph Burckhardt, New York (16, 19); Bevan Davies, New York (24); Deste, London (15); Eeva-Inkeri, New York (Pl. 8); French Government Tourist Office, New York (2); Helga Photo Studio, Inc., New York (22); George Jennings, Jr. (3); Jones-Gessling Studio, Huntington, N.Y. (30); Kulicke Frames, Inc., New York (144); Malcolm Lubliner, Los Angeles (47); M & M Research Engineering, Butler, Wisc. (48); Ed Mayo, Lehigh Press, Pennsauken, N.J. (13); Alexander A. Mirzaoff, Tampa, Fla. (104, 115, 135, 143); Albert L. Mozell, New York (21);

R. Petersen (20); Eric Pollitzer, Hempstead, N.Y. (17, 29, Pls. 5, 9, chapter opening photos); Nick Scheidy, New York (18, 26, 27); Spink & Gaborc, Inc., New York (142); Tetko, Inc., Elmsford, N.Y. (36); John Webb, Cheam, Surrey, England (Pl. 4).

Works by Anuszkiewicz, Barnet, Flack, Lichtenstein, Rauschenberg, Rosenquist, Shahn, Warhol, Wesselman: © V.A.G.A. 1978.

Works by Matisse, Vasarely: © S.P.A.D.E.M. 1978.